Interactive Notebooks

WORD STUDY

Grade 4

Credits
Content Editors: Elise Craver, Angela Triplett

Visit *carsondellosa.com* for correlations to Common Core, state, national, and Canadian provincial standards.

Carson-Dellosa Publishing, LLC
PO Box 35665
Greensboro, NC 27425 USA
carsondellosa.com

978-1-4838-3812-0
01-065177784

Table of Contents

*These lessons include multiple reproducible pages. They are designed to introduce one or more concepts at a time, and can be taught over time. Once assembled, they will use multiple pages in a student's interactive notebook.

What Are Interactive Notebooks?

Interactive notebooks are a unique form of note taking. Teachers guide students through creating pages of notes on new topics. Instead of being in the traditional linear, handwritten format, notes are colorful and spread across the pages. Notes also often include drawings, diagrams, and 3-D elements to make the material understandable and relevant. Students are encouraged to complete their notebook pages in ways that make sense to them. With this personalization, no two pages are exactly the same.

Because of their creative nature, interactive notebooks allow students to be active participants in their own learning. Teachers can easily differentiate pages to address the levels and needs of each learner. The notebooks are arranged sequentially, and students can create tables of contents as they create pages, making it simple for students to use their notebooks for reference throughout the year. The interactive, easily personalized format makes interactive notebooks ideal for engaging students in learning new concepts.

Using interactive notebooks can take as much or as little time as you like. Students will initially take longer to create pages but will get faster as they become familiar with the process of creating pages. You may choose to only create a notebook page as a class at the beginning of each unit, or you may choose to create a new page for each topic within a unit. You can decide what works best for your students and schedule.

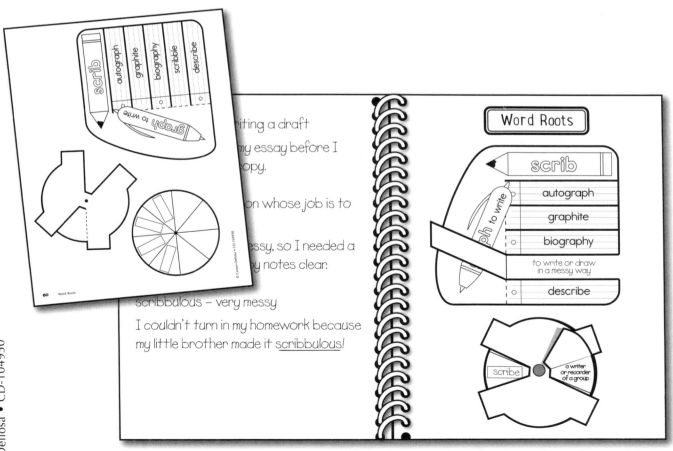

A student's interactive notebook for word roots

Getting Started

You can start using interactive notebooks at any point in the school year. Use the following guidelines to help you get started in your classroom. (For more specific details, management ideas, and tips, see page 10.)

1. Plan each notebook.

Use the planning template (page 9) to lay out a general plan for the topics you plan to cover in each notebook for the year.

2. Choose a notebook type.

Interactive notebooks are usually either single-subject, spiral-bound notebooks, composition books, or three-ring binders with loose-leaf paper. Each type presents pros and cons. See page 5 for a more in-depth look at each type of notebook.

3. Allow students to personalize their notebooks.

Have students decorate their notebook covers, as well as add their names and subjects. This provides a sense of ownership and emphasizes the personalized nature of the notebooks.

4. Number the pages and create the table of contents.

Have students number the bottom outside corner of each page, front and back. When completing a new page, adding a table of contents entry will be easy. Have students title the first page of each notebook "Table of Contents." Have them leave several blank pages at the front of each notebook for the table of contents. Refer to your general plan for an idea of about how many entries students will be creating.

5. Start creating pages.

Always begin a new page by adding an entry to the table of contents. Create the first notebook pages along with students to model proper format and expectations.

This book contains individual topics for you to introduce. Use the pages in the order that best fits your curriculum. You may also choose to alter the content presented to better match your school's curriculum. The provided lesson plans often do not instruct students to add color. Students should make their own choices about personalizing the content in ways that make sense to them. Encourage students to highlight and color the pages as they desire while creating them.

After introducing topics, you may choose to add more practice pages. Use the reproducibles (pages 78–96) to easily create new notebook pages for practice or to introduce topics not addressed in this book.

Use the grading rubric (page 11) to grade students' interactive notebooks at various points throughout the year. Provide students copies of the rubric to glue into their notebooks and refer to as they create pages.

© Carson-Dellosa • CD-104950

What Type of Notebook Should I Use?

Spiral Notebook

The pages in this book are formatted for a standard one-subject notebook.

Pros

- Notebook can be folded in half.
- Page size is larger.
- It is inexpensive.
- It often comes with pockets for storing materials.

Cons

- Pages can easily fall out.
- Spirals can snag or become misshapen.
- Page count and size vary widely.
- It is not as durable as a binder.

Tips

- Encase the spiral in duct tape to make it more durable.
- Keep the notebooks in a central place to prevent them from getting damaged in desks.

Composition Notebook

Pros

- Pages don't easily fall out.
- Page size and page count are standard.
- It is inexpensive.

Cons

- Notebook cannot be folded in half.
- Page size is smaller.
- It is not as durable as a binder.

Tips

- Copy pages meant for standard-sized notebooks at 85 or 90 percent. Test to see which works better for your notebook.

Binder with Loose-Leaf Paper

Pros

- Pages can be easily added, moved, or removed.
- Pages can be removed individually for grading.
- You can add full-page printed handouts.
- It has durable covers.

Cons

- Pages can easily fall out.
- Pages aren't durable.
- It is more expensive than a notebook.
- Students can easily misplace or lose pages.
- Larger size makes it more difficult to store.

Tips

- Provide hole reinforcers for damaged pages.

How to Organize an Interactive Notebook

You may organize an interactive notebook in many different ways. You may choose to organize it by unit and work sequentially through the book. Or, you may choose to create different sections that you will revisit and add to throughout the year. Choose the format that works best for your students and subject.

An interactive notebook includes different types of pages in addition to the pages students create. Non-content pages you may want to add include the following:

Title Page

This page is useful for quickly identifying notebooks. It is especially helpful in classrooms that use multiple interactive notebooks for different subjects. Have students write the subject (such as "Word Study") on the title page of each interactive notebook. They should also include their full names. You may choose to have them include other information such as the teacher's name, classroom number, or class period.

Table of Contents

The table of contents is an integral part of the interactive notebook. It makes referencing previously created pages quick and easy for students. Make sure that students leave several pages at the beginning of each notebook for a table of contents.

Expectations and Grading Rubric

It is helpful for each student to have a copy of the expectations for creating interactive notebook pages. You may choose to include a list of expectations for parents and students to sign, as well as a grading rubric (page 11).

Unit Title Pages

Consider using a single page at the beginning of each section to separate it. Title the page with the unit name. Add a tab (page 78) to the edge of the page to make it easy to flip to the unit. Add a table of contents for only the pages in that unit.

Glossary

Reserve a six-page section at the back of the notebook where students can create a glossary. Draw a line to split in half the front and back of each page, creating 24 sections. Combine *Q* and *R* and *Y* and *Z* to fit the entire alphabet. Have students add an entry as each new vocabulary word is introduced.

Formatting Student Notebook Pages

The other major consideration for planning an interactive notebook is how to treat the left and right sides of a notebook spread. Interactive journals are usually viewed with the notebook open flat. This creates a left side and a right side. You have several options for how to treat the two sides of the spread.

Traditionally, the right side is used for the teacher-directed part of the lesson, and the left side is used for students to interact with the lesson content. The lessons in this book use this format. However, you may prefer to switch the order for your class so that the teacher-directed learning is on the left and the student input is on the right.

It can also be important to include standards, learning objectives, or essential questions in interactive notebooks. You may choose to write these on the top-left side of each page before completing the teacher-directed page on the right side. You may also choose to have students include the "Introduction" part of each lesson in that same top-left section. This is the *in, through, out* method. Students enter *in* the lesson on the top left of the page, go *through* the lesson on the right page, and exit *out* of the lesson on the bottom left with a reflection activity.

The following chart details different types of items and activities that you could include on each side.

Left Side	Right Side
• learning objectives	• vocabulary and definitions
• essential questions	• mini-lessons
• I Can statements	• folding activities
• brainstorming	• steps in a process
• making connections	• example problems
• summarizing	• notes
• making conclusions	• diagrams
• practice problems	• graphic organizers
• opinions	• hints and tips
• questions	• big ideas
• mnemonics	
• drawings and diagrams	

Planning for the Year

Making a general plan for interactive notebooks will help with planning, grading, and testing throughout the year. You do not need to plan every single page, but knowing what topics you will cover and in what order can be helpful in many ways.

Use the Interactive Notebook Plan (page 9) to plan your units and topics and where they should be placed in the notebooks. Remember to include enough pages at the beginning for the non-content pages, such as the title page, table of contents, and grading rubric. You may also want to leave a page at the beginning of each unit to place a mini table of contents for just that section.

In addition, when planning new pages, it can be helpful to sketch the pieces you will need to create. Use the following notebook template and notes to plan new pages.

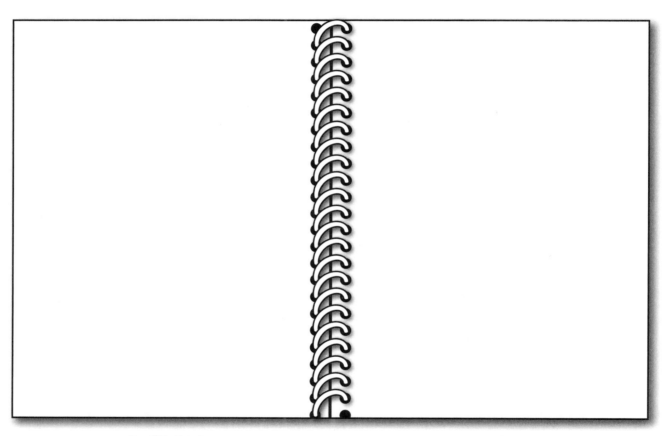

Left Side   **Right Side**

Notes

_____

_____

_____

Interactive Notebook Plan

Page	Topic	Page	Topic
1		51	
2		52	
3		53	
4		54	
5		55	
6		56	
7		57	
8		58	
9		59	
10		60	
11		61	
12		62	
13		63	
14		64	
15		65	
16		66	
17		67	
18		68	
19		69	
20		70	
21		71	
22		72	
23		73	
24		74	
25		75	
26		76	
27		77	
28		78	
29		79	
30		80	
31		81	
32		82	
33		83	
34		84	
35		85	
36		86	
37		87	
38		88	
39		89	
40		90	
41		91	
42		92	
43		93	
44		94	
45		95	
46		96	
47		97	
48		98	
49		99	
50		100	

Managing Interactive Notebooks in the Classroom

Working with Younger Students

- Use your yearly plan to preprogram a table of contents that you can copy and give to students to glue into their notebooks, instead of writing individual entries.

- Have assistants or parent volunteers precut pieces.

- Create glue sponges to make gluing easier. Place large sponges in plastic containers with white glue. The sponges will absorb the glue. Students can wipe the backs of pieces across the sponges to apply the glue with less mess.

Creating Notebook Pages

- For storing loose pieces, add a pocket to the inside back cover. Use the envelope pattern (page 81), an envelope, a jumbo library pocket, or a resealable plastic bag. Or, tape the bottom and side edges of the two last pages of the notebook together to create a large pocket.

- When writing under flaps, have students trace the outline of each flap so that they can visualize the writing boundary.

- Where the dashed line will be hidden on the inside of the fold, have students first fold the piece in the opposite direction so that they can see the dashed line. Then, students should fold the piece back the other way along the same fold line to create the fold in the correct direction.

- To avoid losing pieces, have students keep all of their scraps on their desks until they have finished each page.

- To contain paper scraps and avoid multiple trips to the trash can, provide small groups with small buckets or tubs.

- For students who run out of room, keep full and half sheets available. Students can glue these to the bottom of the pages and fold them up when not in use.

Dealing with Absences

- Create a model notebook for absent students to reference when they return to school.

- Have students cut a second set of pieces as they work on their own pages.

Using the Notebook

- To organize sections of the notebook, provide each student with a sheet of tabs (page 78).

- To easily find the next blank page, either cut off the top-right corner of each page as it is used or attach a long piece of yarn or ribbon to the back cover to be used as a bookmark.

Interactive Notebook Grading Rubric

4

_____ Table of contents is complete.

_____ All notebook pages are included.

_____ All notebook pages are complete.

_____ Notebook pages are neat and organized.

_____ Information is correct.

_____ Pages show personalization, evidence of learning, and original ideas.

3

_____ Table of contents is mostly complete.

_____ One notebook page is missing.

_____ Notebook pages are mostly complete.

_____ Notebook pages are mostly neat and organized.

_____ Information is mostly correct.

_____ Pages show some personalization, evidence of learning, and original ideas.

2

_____ Table of contents is missing a few entries.

_____ A few notebook pages are missing.

_____ A few notebook pages are incomplete.

_____ Notebook pages are somewhat messy and unorganized.

_____ Information has several errors.

_____ Pages show little personalization, evidence of learning, or original ideas.

1

_____ Table of contents is incomplete.

_____ Many notebook pages are missing.

_____ Many notebook pages are incomplete.

_____ Notebook pages are too messy and unorganized to use.

_____ Information is incorrect.

_____ Pages show no personalization, evidence of learning, or original ideas.

Practicing High Frequency Words

Introduction

Explain that high frequency words are words that appear frequently in text. Introduce each new high frequency word by writing it on the board. Say the word several times with the class. Have volunteers define each word and use it in a sentence. Finally, discuss any identifying features students see in the words, such as affixes, roots, or spelling patterns. Discuss how categorizing high frequency words by word parts or spelling patterns can also be helpful in learning the words quickly.

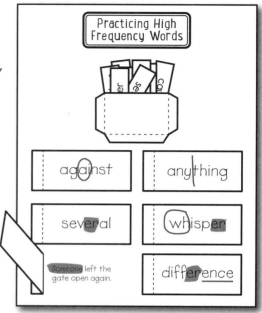

Creating the Notebook Page

Guide students through the following steps to complete the right-hand page in their notebooks.

1. Add a Table of Contents entry for the Practicing High Frequency Words pages.

2. Cut out the title and glue it to the top of the page.

3. Cut out the pocket. Apply glue to the backs of the three tabs and attach the pocket to the page below the title.

4. Cut out the flaps. Apply glue to the backs of the left sections and attach them to the page below the pocket.

5. Cut out the word cards. Store the cards in the pocket.

6. For each flap, choose a word card from the pocket. Write the word on the front of the flap. Then, dissect the word by highlighting the affixes and root or identifying the word's spelling pattern(s). Write a sentence with the word under the flap. Highlight the word in the sentence.

7. Pull additional words out of the pocket and practice reading and writing them. If desired, use self-stick notes to create additional word study flaps as used in step 6 on additional pages.

Reflect on Learning

To complete the left-hand page, have students choose several more word cards from the pocket to dissect. Then, students should write a sentence with each word. Have the students read their sentences with a partner.

Practicing High Frequency Words

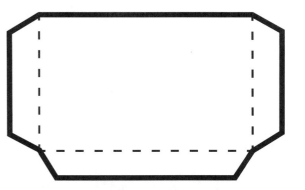

afraid	against	anything
brought	caught	compare
difference	hungry	interest
receive	remember	several
someone	themselves	whisper

awhile	daily	develop
experience	heavy	instead
listen	possible	quiet
quite	solution	station
straight	suppose	though

century	condition	create
decision	dependent	figure
frighten	herself	himself
material	raise	rough
sincerely	special	through

Using High Frequency Words

Introduction

Copy and distribute a story (or pages from a story) that uses the high frequency words that the class has been working with. Have students take turns reading the story aloud. Then, have students find and highlight the high frequency words used in the text.

Creating the Notebook Page

Guide students through the following steps to complete the right-hand page in their notebooks.

happened	during	remember
complete	however	listen
piece	several	measure
discover	animals	nothing
money	fall	problem
map	ground	today
morning	covered	everything
		easy
		fast

1. Add a Table of Contents entry for the Using High Frequency Words pages.

2. Cut out the title and glue it to the top of the page.

3. Cut out the square piece. With the printed side up, fold it in half so that the opposite corners meet, then unfold. Repeat with the other two corners. You should have an X-shaped fold. Flip the paper over so that the blank side is faceup. Fold each corner in to meet the center. You should have a square piece with four triangular flaps. Flip the paper over again so that the opposite side is faceup. Fold each corner in to meet the center. You should have a smaller square with four triangular flaps. Fold the bottom edge up to meet the top edge to create a rectangular fortune teller.

4. Place your thumbs and forefingers of both hands under the four square flaps. Gently press your fingers together toward the center so the four corners meet in the center and the piece becomes 3-D. It may be helpful to have a friend press down on the center during this step.

5. Cut out the pocket. Apply glue to the backs of the three tabs and attach the pocket to the page below the title. Use the pocket to store the flattened fortune teller when not in use.

6. To use the fortune teller to practice high frequency words, choose one of the four visible words. Say the word and spell it. For each letter, close and open the fortune teller once, making sure to alternate directions. (Your fingers will alternate so that your thumbs meet and your forefingers meet, then each thumb meets a forefinger.) Repeat with the next set of words. The third time, say and spell a word from the center of the fortune teller, but don't move the fortune teller. After spelling the third word, open the flap to read your "fortune." Identify the high frequency words in the fortune.

7. During each turn, identify the high frequency words used from beginning to end and record them on the page to practice spelling them.

Reflect on Learning

To complete the left-hand page, have students use their high frequency word lists to write several fortunes of their own. Students should highlight the high frequency words they used in their fortunes.

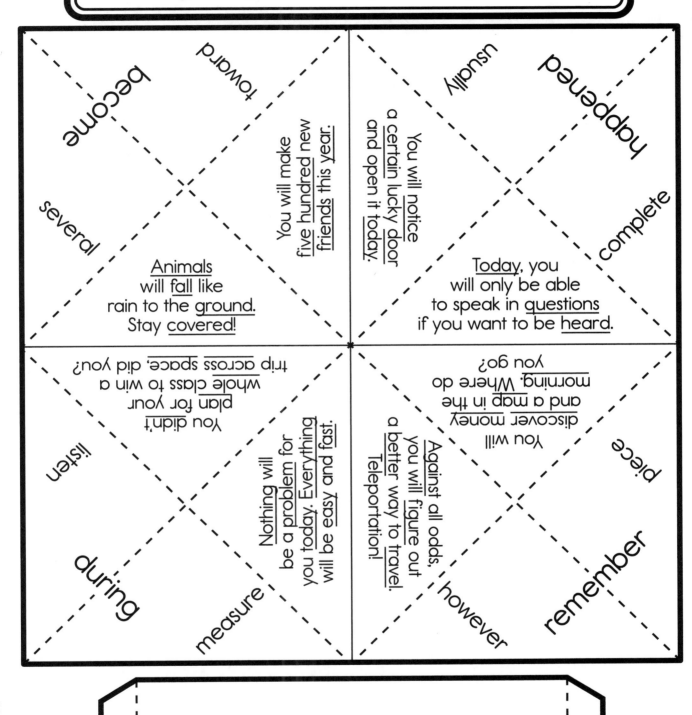

become

toward

usually

happened

several

complete

You will make
five hundred new
friends this year.

You will notice
a certain lucky door
and open it today.

Animals
will fall like
rain to the ground.
Stay covered!

Today, you
will only be able
to speak in questions
if you want to be heard.

You didn't
plan for your
whole class to win a
trip across space, did you?

You will
discover money
and a map in the
morning. Where do
you go?

listen

Nothing will
be a problem for
you today. Everything
will be easy and fast.

Against all odds,
you will figure out
a better way to travel.
Teleportation!

piece

during

measure

however

remember

Words with *R*-Controlled Vowels

Introduction

Write the words *birthday* and *fireplace* on the board. Have students read the two words aloud. Then, write *mature* and *purpose* on the board. Have students say the new words. Discuss how the vowel sound changes in each pair of words, even though both vowel sounds are followed by the consonant *r*. Finally, have students notice the difference in the movement of their mouths when saying each pair of words.

Creating the Notebook Page

Guide students through the following steps to complete the right-hand page in their notebooks.

1. Add a Table of Contents entry for the Words with *R*-Controlled Vowels pages.

2. Cut out the title and glue it to the top of the page.

3. Cut out the pockets. Apply glue to the backs of the three tabs on each pocket and attach them to the page, leaving enough room above each pocket for adding word cards.

4. Cut out the word cards.

5. Fold the picture behind the word on the dashed line. Apply glue to the back of the picture section and attach it to the back of the word to create a double-sided card with a picture on the front and a word on the back.

6. Look at the picture on each card and say the word. Listen to the vowel sound. Sort the word into the correct pocket. Discuss how some *r*-controlled vowels make the same sound.

7. Look at the words in each pocket. Write the *r*-controlled vowel in the blank on the word card. You may need to re-sort some of the words. If needed, use a dictionary to find the correct spelling.

8. To practice spelling *r*-controlled words, remove all of the cards and place them picture-side up. Try spelling the word. Look at the word on the back of the card to check your spelling. If you are correct, sort the word into the corresponding pocket. Repeat until all of the words have been sorted correctly.

Reflect on Learning

To complete the left-hand page, have students divide their pages into two sections and label each section *R-Controlled* and *Not R-Controlled*. Say several words, including some *r*-controlled vowel words. Students should write each word correctly in the corresponding column as you say them.

Words with R-Controlled Vowels

ar

er ir or ur

batt__er__y	c__or__cle	diction__ar__y	E__ar__th	imp__or__tant	p__er__fect	th__ir__teen	weath__er__	wr__o__m
(battery)	◯	(dictionary)	(Earth)	i — This is imp__tant!	100% is a ___ score.	13	(weather)	(worm)
anch__or__	b__ir__thday	c__er__tains	d__or__ty	he__ar__t	Janu__ar__y	p__ie__chase	Th__ur__sday	wond__er__ful
(anchor)	(cake)	A	(pig)	♥	___ February, March	(purchase)	Wednesday, ___ Friday	That's wond__full!

Vowel Teams

Introduction

Write the words *author* and *flawless* on the board. Have students say the words aloud. Discuss how the /aw/ vowel team makes the same sound but the words are spelled differently. Have volunteers write more words with the /aw/ vowel team on the board. Review the vowel teams *ea* and *oo*, and the sets of vowel teams for /oy/, /ew/, and /ow/ and repeat the activity. Then, assign different vowel teams to groups of students. Have each group find and list as many words as possible with their vowel team in a specified amount of time.

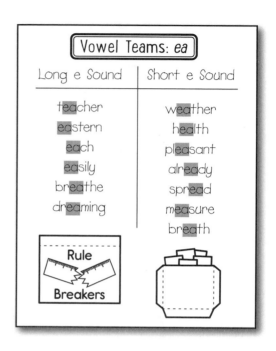

Creating the Notebook Page

Guide students through the following steps to complete the right-hand page in their notebooks.

1. Add a Table of Contents entry for the Vowel Teams pages.

2. Cut out the title and glue it to the top of the page.

3. Cut out the pocket. Apply glue to the backs of the three tabs and attach the pocket to the bottom-right side of the page.

4. If there is a *Rule Breakers* flap, cut it out. Apply glue to the back of the top section and attach it to the bottom-left side of the page.

5. Cut out the word cards. Read the word on each card, listening for the differences in vowel sounds. If there is a difference, sort the words by vowel sound. If the vowel sounds are all the same, sort the words by spelling pattern. Place words that do not fit any pattern on the *Rule Breakers* flap.

6. Decide on the headings for the sorted words (for example, the spelling pattern, or the sound of the vowel team). Write the headings on the page below the title and draw dividing lines to create a T-chart. Say the word on each card. Then, write the word under the correct column or under the *Rule Breakers* flap. Store the word cards in the pocket.

Reflect on Learning

To complete the left-hand page, write several words with vowel teams on the board such as *proof, greasy, crawl, cashew,* and *oyster.* Have students copy the first word on the left-hand side of the page. Students should look at the word, then cover the word by folding the left-hand edge of the paper over the word. Erase the word from the board. Have students write the word next to the covered word, then check the spelling by uncovering the correctly written word.

Vowel Teams: *oo*

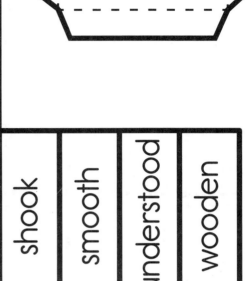

cocoon	bookcase
footprint	cookie
harpoon	goodbye
kangaroo	hoof
monsoon	lagoon
noodle	moody
shampoo	overlook
	shook
	smooth
	understood
	wooden

Vowel Teams: *ea*

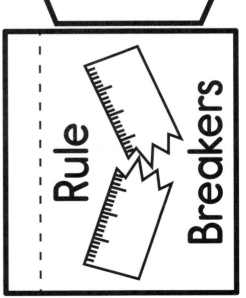

Rule Breakers

breath	already
dreaming	breathe
easily	each
great	eastern
measure	health
spread	pleasant
weather	teacher

Vowel Teams: /aw/

audience	author	awesome	awful	because	brawny	caution
daughter	dawdle	flawless	gnaw	laugh	laundry	vault

Rule Breakers

Vowel Teams: /ew/

balloon	bruise	chews	choose	cruise	jewel	juice
lawsuit	nephew	quiet	review	school	spooky	unhook

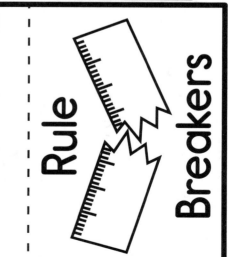

Rule Breakers

Vowel Teams: /oy/

annoy	avoid	choice	convoy	decoy	destroy	disappoint

disloyal	employer	enjoy	joint	moisture	oily	poison	royal	spoil	voice	voyage

Vowel Teams: /ow/

allow	could	counter	country	coward	crowd	doubtful

flower	fountain	mountain	prowler	scoundrel	thousand	vowel

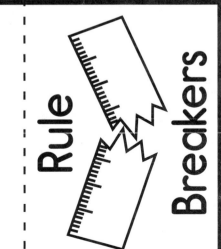

Rule Breakers

Pronouncing "ough"

Introduction

Write the following sentence on the board: *Have you thought this through thoroughly enough?* Have a volunteer read the sentence aloud. Circle each -*ough* word in the sentence. Discuss the different sounds the -*ough* makes in the words in the sentence. Write a word that rhymes with each circled word in the sentence below the word.

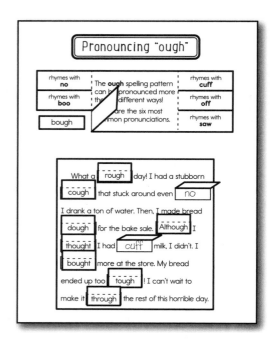

Creating the Notebook Page

Guide students through the following steps to complete the right-hand page in their notebooks.

1. Add a Table of Contents entry for the Pronouncing "ough" pages.

2. Cut out the title and glue it to the top of the page.

3. Cut out the six-flap flap book. Cut on the solid lines to create six flaps. Apply glue to the back of the center section and attach it to the page below the title.

4. Cut out the six word cards. Discuss the different sounds *ough* can make. Glue the correct rhyming *ough* word under each flap as an example.

5. Cut out the paragraph piece and glue it to the bottom of the page.

6. Cut out the 10 word flaps. Read the paragraph and place the correct word flap in each blank space. Once all of the flaps have been placed correctly, apply glue to the backs of the top sections and glue them in place.

7. Under each flap, write a clue to the pronunciation, such as a rhyming word from the flap book at the top of the page.

8. With a partner, practice reading the paragraph and pronouncing the *ough* words correctly.

Reflect on Learning

To complete the left-hand page, have students divide their page into two columns labeled *ough* and *Not ough*. Say several *ough* and non-*ough* words, such as *rough, bought, cuff, thought, row*, etc. Have students record the words in the corresponding columns, being sure to spell them correctly.

Answer Key:
What a rough day! I had a stubborn cough that stuck around even though I drank a ton of water. Then, I made bread dough for the bake sale. Although I thought I had enough milk, I didn't. I bought more at the store. My bread ended up too tough! I can't wait to make it through the rest of this horrible day.

Pronouncing "ough"

Although	bought

	The **ough** spelling pattern can be pronounced more than 10 different ways!	
rhymes with **no**		rhymes with **cuff**
rhymes with **boo**		rhymes with **off**
rhymes with **how**	These are the six most common pronunciations.	rhymes with **saw**

bough	bought	cough
dough	rough	through

What a [   ] day! I had a stubborn

[   ] that stuck around even [   ]

I drank a ton of water. Then, I made bread

[   ] for the bake sale. [   ] I

[   ] I had [   ] milk, I didn't. I

[   ] more at the store. My bread

ended up too [   ]! I can't wait to

make it [   ] the rest of this horrible day.

cough
dough
enough
rough
though
thought
through
tough

Spelling: The /k/ Sound

Write the words *squeak, brick, plaque,* and *shake* on the board. Say the words aloud with the class. Ask students if they have ever wondered why the /k/ sound is spelled differently in each word and how they know which spelling to use. Explain that looking for patterns in words with the same /k/ spelling can help them choose the correct spelling with unknown words. Brainstorm other words with the /k/ sound with the class and list them on the board. Have volunteers come to the board and circle the /k/ sound in each word. Then, sort the words by their /k/ spelling patterns. Have students begin to look for patterns in the groups of words.

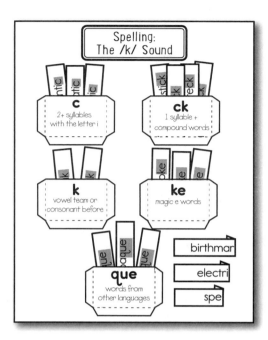

Creating the Notebook Page

Guide students through the following steps to complete the right-hand page in their notebooks.

1. Add a Table of Contents entry for the Spelling: The /k/ Sound pages.

2. Cut out the title and glue it to the top of the page.

3. Cut out the five pockets. Apply glue to the backs of the three tabs on each pocket and glue them to the page, leaving enough room above each pocket for adding word cards.

4. Cut out the word cards. Underline or highlight the /k/ spelling pattern in each word. Sort them into the corresponding pockets by the spelling of the /k/ sound.

5. Look at all of the words in one pocket and look for patterns. Decide on a rule and write it on the pocket below the spelling pattern. (Rules may include: *c* is used in multisyllabic words and with *i*; *ck* is used in one-syllable words; *k* is used with vowel teams and consonants; *ke* is used in CVe words; and *que* is used in words from other languages.)

6. To practice choosing the correct spelling, read each word aloud and find the /k/ sound. Fold the word card so that the /k/ spelling in the word is hidden. For example, fold between the *i* and the *q* in *antique* so that it shows *anti,* and *que* is folded behind. Read the folded words and place them in the correct pockets. Check your work by unfolding the cards in each pocket.

Reflect on Learning

To complete the left-hand page, have students divide their pages into sections labeled *c, que, ck, k,* and *ke.* Then, have students look through magazines and books to find words with the /k/ sound. Have them write words in the correct sections. Students should highlight the /k/ sound in each word.

Spelling: The /k/ Sound

authentic	artichoke	antique
croak	candlestick	birthmark
magic	electric	dramatic
pluck	opaque	mistake
shipwreck	shack	quake
unique	speck	sleek

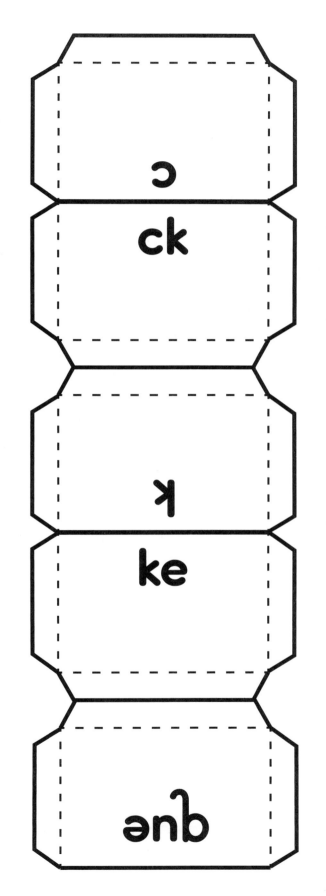

c

ck

k

ke

que

Spelling: -*ion*

Introduction

Write the words *pollution*, *action*, and *confession* on the board. Discuss the similar ending /shun/ sound in each word and how it is spelled. Explain that the most common way to spell the /shun/ sound is -*tion*. However, when the letters *l*, *r*, and *s* come before the sound, the words are spelled with -*sion* instead.

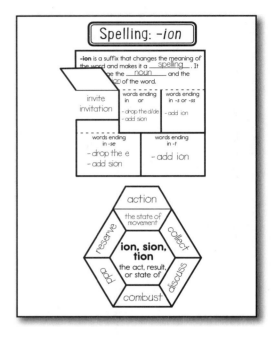

Creating the Notebook Page

Guide students through the following steps to complete the right-hand page in their notebooks.

1. Add a Table of Contents entry for the Spelling: -*ion* pages.

2. Cut out the title and glue it to the top of the page.

3. Cut out the three-flap book. Cut on the solid lines to create three flaps. Apply glue to the back of the top section and attach it to the page below the title.

4. Cut out the two-flap book. Cut on the solid line to create two flaps. Apply glue to the back of the top section and attach it to the page below the top flap book. If desired, place the top section under the three flaps on the top flap book to make a single five-flap book.

5. Complete the explanation. (-*ion* is a suffix that changes the meaning of the word and makes it a **noun**. It can change the **spelling** and the **pronunciation** of the word.)

6. On each flap, write the spelling rule. Discuss how there may be exceptions to each rule. Under each flap, write an example word pair (see Answer Key for rules and example words).

7. Cut out the hexagon flap book. Fold the flaps toward the center on the dashed lines. Apply glue to the back of the center section and attach it to the bottom of the page.

8. On each flap, write a base word or root. Under each flap, write the related -*ion* word on the top section and the definition on the bottom section.

Reflect on Learning

To complete the left-hand page, write several words on the board with the *t* or *s* missing before the -*ion* such as *connec_ion*, *lo_ion*, or *express_ion*. Have students write *t* or *s* to complete the word correctly and use the dictionary to check their spellings.

Answer Key
Ending in *e*: drop the *e*, add -*ation*, invite, invitation; Ending in *d/de*: drop the *d/de*, add -*sion*, explode, explosion; Ending in *s/ss*: add -*ion*, discuss, discussion; Ending in *se*: drop the *e*, add -*sion*, televise, television; Ending in *nt*, *pt*, *rt*, and *st*: add -*ion*, act, action

Spelling: -ion

-ion is a suffix that changes the meaning of the word and makes it a _____ . It can change the _____ and the _____ of the word.

words ending in -e	words ending in -d or -de	words ending in -s or -ss

words ending in -t

words ending in -se

ion, sion, tion

the act, result, or state of

Spelling: -*able* and -*ible*

Introduction

Write words ending in -*able* and -*ible* on index cards. Divide students into small groups and give each group a set of index cards. Have the groups decide on a way to sort the words. Then, have each group explain their thinking. Finally, have groups find and share any patterns within their groups.

Both suffixes -**able** and -**ible** mean _able_

But, which do yo

Tip 1

If the root is a complete word, it usually uses _able_

depend|able

ible

incred|ible

read|able

respons | accent | non | convert

Creating the Notebook Page

Guide students through the following steps to complete the right-hand page in their notebooks.

1. Add a Table of Contents entry for the Spelling: -*able* and -*ible* pages.

2. Cut out the title and glue it to the top of the page.

3. Cut out the flap book. Cut on the solid line to create two flaps. Apply glue to the back of the left section and attach it to the page below the title.

4. Complete the definition. (Both suffixes -*able* and -*ible* mean **able to be**.)

5. Cut out the ___ *is more common* and *If the root . . .* pieces. Glue them under the *Tip 1* and *Tip 2* flaps.

6. Complete and discuss the tips. (-**able** is more common. If the root is a complete word, it usually uses -**able**.) Explain that all other words end in -*ible*.

7. Cut out the pocket. Apply glue to the backs of the tabs and attach the pocket to the bottom of the page.

8. Cut out the eight word cards. Store them in the pocket.

9. Cut out the *able* and *ible* pieces. Glue them to the middle of the page.

10. Fold each word card immediately after the end of the word. Hold the folded card beside the *able* and *ible* pieces to figure out which is the correct ending (use the tips in the flap book above as needed). Unfold the piece and write the correct ending on the word card.

Reflect on Learning

To complete the left-hand page, write several additional words such as *calculate*, *advise*, and *forget* on the board. Have students correctly write the words with the -*able* or -*ible* suffix. Students should record the rule they used for converting the word beside each word. For example, removing the suffix from a base word (*calculate*, *calculable*), dropping the *e* (*advise*, *advisable*) or doubling consonants (*forget*, *forgettable*).

Spelling: -*able* and -*ible*

| Both suffixes **-able** and **-ible** mean _____ . But, which do you use? | **Tip 1** |
| | **Tip 2** |

_____ is more common.

If the root is a complete word, it usually uses _____.

able	ible

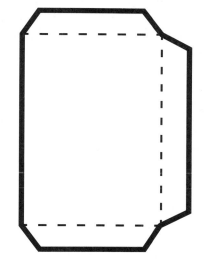

accept	convert
depend	horr
incred	like
read	respons

Syllables

Introduction

Review syllables. Discuss how in a closed syllable, the vowel is followed by a consonant. Write the word *gossip* on the board. Have students say the word. Show how the vowel is "closed in" by the consonant in each syllable. The vowel has a short vowel sound when it is "closed in." Write the word *unite* on the board. Show how the vowel in each syllable is "open" and is not closed in by a consonant. Open vowels have long vowel sounds. Review several more examples of words with open and closed syllables on the board. Explain that in some syllables, the vowel has the schwa sound (/uh/) instead, and caution them to look for these exceptions.

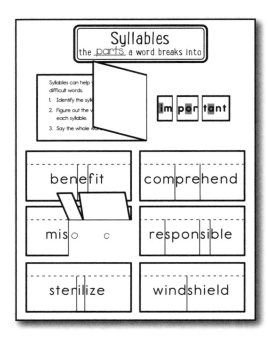

Creating the Notebook Page

Guide students through the following steps to complete the right-hand page in their notebooks.

1. Add a Table of Contents entry for the Syllables pages.

2. Cut out the title and glue it to the top of the page.

3. Complete the definition (the **parts** a word breaks into).

4. Cut out the *Syllables can help you read more difficult words* piece. Apply glue to the back of the left section and attach it to the page below the title.

5. Cut out the *important* word card. Cut the word card apart into syllables. Apply glue to the back of each syllable piece and attach them under the *1 syllable = 1 vowel sound* flap.

6. Identify the vowel sound in each syllable of *important* by highlighting it or circling it.

7. Cut out the flaps. Identify the syllables in each word. Cut the word between each syllable to create a flap book with two or more flaps. Apply glue to the back of the top section of each flap and attach them to the page.

8. Review the difference between open and closed syllables. Write *O* (open syllable) or *C* (closed syllable) under each cut flap to identify the syllable type. If desired, highlight the syllables with the schwa sound.

Reflect on Learning

To complete the left-hand page, have students write several correctly spelled multisyllabic words in their notebooks. Then, have students exchange notebooks with a partner. Each partner should divide the words into syllables and mark the syllables as *O* (open) or *C* (closed).

Syllables

the _____ a word breaks into

important

Syllables can help you read more difficult words.

1. Identify the syllables.
2. Figure out the vowel sound in each syllable.
3. Say the whole word.

1 **syllable**
=
1 **vowel sound**

---

benefit	comprehend
mistaken	responsible
sterilize	windshield

Syllabication Rules

Review syllabication. Write several familiar words on the board and have students say the words and count the syllables. Write *centralization* on the board. As a class, work together to count the syllables and pronounce the words. Emphasize that there is one vowel sound per syllable. Repeat with several other difficult words.

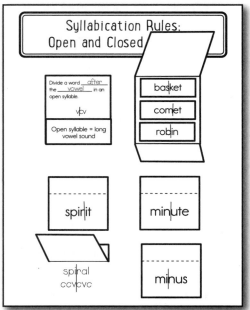

Creating the Notebook Page

Guide students through the following steps to complete the right-hand page in their notebooks.

1. Add a Table of Contents entry for the Syllabication Rules pages.

2. Cut out the title and glue it to the top of the page.

3. Cut out the two trifolds. For each one, fold the top and bottom flaps towards the blank side on the dashed lines, so that the smaller flap overlaps the larger flap. Apply glue to the gray glue section on the back and attach the trifolds to the page below the title.

4. Complete the explanations on each trifold. Draw a line to divide the example. (See Answer Key.)

5. Cut out the six word cards. Draw lines to divide each into syllables. Decide which syllable rule best describes the word and glue it inside the related trifold.

6. Cut out the two sets of word flaps. Draw lines to divide each word into syllables. Discuss how the syllabication rule affects the pronunciation of similar words. Match each pair to the related syllabication rule. Apply glue to the backs of the top sections and attach them to the page below the corresponding trifold.

7. Under each flap, rewrite the word and label it to show the syllabication rule. For example, label the consonants and vowels and show the syllable division.

Reflect on Learning

To complete the left-hand page, have students explain in their own words how each syllabication rule affects reading, writing, and pronouncing words. Have students include example words as evidence.

Answer Key
Open syllable: Divide a word **after** the **vowel** in an open syllable V/CV; Closed syllable: Divide a word **after** the **consonant** in a closed syllable. VC/V; *R*-controlled: often found at the **end** of…, not a **long** or a **short** vowel sound, VC/er; VCe: **one** syllable, may include a **consonant**, **blend**, or **digraph**, C/VCe; Double consonant: divide **between** double consonants…at the **end** of a word, they're a **digraph**, or…a **base** word, VC/CV; Consonant digraphs/blends: do not **divide**…, CVCC/VCC; C + *le*: only found at the **end** of…, separate a **consonant** from the *le*, V/Cle; Compound words: divide **between** the two words, …more than **one** syllable…, CVC/CVC; Prefixes: divide **after** the prefix, …more than **one** syllable…, pre/fix; Suffixes: divide **before** the suffix, …more than **one** syllable…, suffix/es

© Carson-Dellosa • CD-104950

Syllabication Rules: Open and Closed Syllables

Open syllable = long vowel sound

glue

Divide a word _____ the _____ in an open syllable.

VCV

Closed syllable = short vowel sound

glue

Divide a word _____ the _____ in a closed syllable.

VCV

apron

basket

comet

lady

robin

zebra

minus | minute

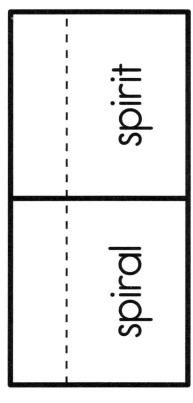

spirit

spiral

Syllabication Rules: Vowel Patterns

r-controlled vowel = one syllable

glue

- often found at the _____ of multiple-syllable words
- not a _____ or a _____ vowel sound

VCVr

VCe = long vowel sound

glue

- _____ syllable
- may include a _____, _____, or _____

CVCe

birthday

compose

farmyard

grapevine

parade

tutor

dividend

divide

concert | concept

Syllabication Rules: Letter Pairs

double consonant = two syllables (usually)

glue

- divide _____ double consonants
- unless they're at the _____ of a word
- they're a _____ , or
- they're part of a _____ word

VCCV

consonant digraph/blend = one syllable

glue

- do not _____ a consonant blend or digraph

CVCCVCC

cinnamon

checkers

hiccup

marching

nesting

suddenly

restrain

restless

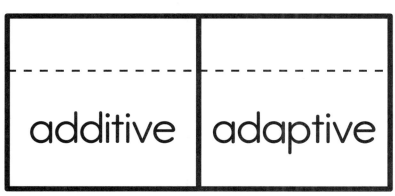

additive | adaptive

Syllabication Rules:
C + le and Compound Words

C + le = one syllable

glue

- only found at the
  _____ of words
- do not separate a
  _____ from the le

VCle

---

compound words = two
or more syllables

glue

- divide _____
  the two words
- there may be more
  than _____
  syllable in each base
  word

CVCCVC

---

candlestick

coffeepot

drizzle

example

moonlight

pickle

---

inside | insist

---

tablet

table

Syllabication Rules: Prefixes and Suffixes

prefix = one syllable

glue

- divide _____ the prefix

- there may be more than _____ syllable in the prefix

prefix

suffix = one syllable

glue

- divide _____ the suffix

- there may be more than _____ syllable in the suffix

suffixes

disrespect

drinkable

enjoyment

subtitles

talkative

undercover

unicycle

unit

teacher | another

Stressed and Unstressed Syllables

Introduction

Say a common two-syllable word, such as *elbow*. Repeat the word several times, switching the stress each time: EL-bow, el-BOW. Repeat with several more words and have students listen and identify which stress pattern sounds correct for each word. Then, have students choose a simple word and try to switch the stress. Explain that multisyllabic words have correct stress patterns that help readers understand and say the words correctly.

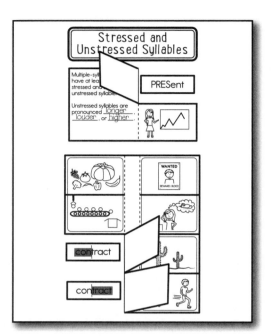

Creating the Notebook Page

Guide students through the following steps to complete the right-hand page in their notebooks.

1. Add a Table of Contents entry for the Stressed and Unstressed Syllables pages.

2. Cut out the title and glue it to the top of the page.

3. Cut out the *Multiple-syllable words . . .* flap book. Cut on the solid line to create two flaps. Apply glue to the back of the left section and attach it to the page below the title.

4. Complete the explanation. (Multiple-syllable words have at least **one** stressed and **one** unstressed syllable. Unstressed syllables are pronounced **longer**, **louder**, or **higher**.)

5. Cut out the *PREsent/preSENT* cards. Read each card with the stress on the capitalized syllable. Then, glue each card under the matching picture flap. Discuss how the stress of the syllable affects meaning. If desired, introduce the stress symbol (´) and have students draw it on the word cards to indicate the stressed syllable.

6. Cut out the eight-flap flap book. Cut on the solid lines to create eight flaps. Apply glue to the back of the center section and attach it to the page.

7. Cut out the word cards.

8. Read each word card. Glue each card under the matching picture flap. For example, glue *produce* and *produce* under the flaps with pictures of fruits and vegetables and a conveyor belt. Draw lines to divide each word into syllables. Then, draw the stress symbol over the stressed syllable or highlight the stressed syllable in each word so that it shows the pronunciation that matches the picture.

Reflect on Learning

To complete the left-hand page, have students write names that are important to them, such as their own first, middle, and last name, their school name, their teacher's name, their state name, etc. Then, have them divide each word into syllables and mark or highlight each accented syllable.

Stressed and Unstressed Syllables

Multiple-syllable words have at least _____ stressed and _____ unstressed syllable.

Unstressed syllables are pronounced _____, _____, or _____.

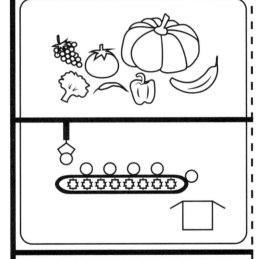

presENT

PRESent

suspect

suspect

produce

produce

desert

desert

contract

contract

Using Stressed and Unstressed Syllables

Introduction

Read the following sentence to the class, using the incorrect stress as marked: *The kitTEN was racING after the UNraveling ball of rainBOW colored fuzZY yarn.* Discuss how the sentence sounded and why. Explain that in multisyllabic words, often the first or second syllable is stressed, and that giving a word the wrong stress can affect understanding and fluent reading.

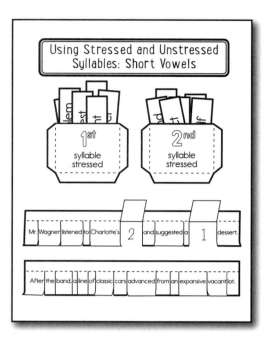

Creating the Notebook Page

Guide students through the following steps to complete the right-hand page in their notebooks.

1. Add a Table of Contents entry for the Using Stressed and Unstressed Syllables pages.

2. Cut out the title and glue it to the top of the page.

3. Cut out the pockets. Apply glue to the backs of the three tabs and attach the pockets to the page below the title, leaving enough room above them to insert word cards.

4. Cut out the word cards.

5. Read each word. Draw lines on the card to divide the word into syllables. Discuss how to identify the stressed syllable in each word. Provide several methods, such as saying the word with the stress on different syllables to find what sounds right, placing a hand underneath your chin to see what syllable moves your jaw the farthest, or saying it naturally in a sentence and listening for the stress. Mark or highlight the stressed syllable on each word card. Then, sort the words into the correct pockets, based on the stressed syllable.

6. Cut out the two flaps. Cut vertically into the flap to separate the sentence into words (one flap per word). Apply glue to the backs of the top sections and attach them to the bottom of the page. Glue the flaps with one-syllable words to the page.

7. Under the flaps of the remaining words, write *1* if the stress is on the first syllable, or *2* if the stress is on the second syllable. Then, practice reading the sentence fluently.

Reflect on Learning

To complete the left-hand page, provide students with a short poem that contains rhythm to glue in their notebooks. Explain that poems often rely on stress to create rhythm. Challenge students to identify the stressed and unstressed words and syllables in each line. Have students describe the rhythm of the poem.

Using Stressed and Unstressed Syllables: Short Vowels

1st syllable stressed

2nd syllable stressed

collect	absent
escape	demand
forgot	exit
honest	herself
pretend	office
travel	problem

Mr. Wagner listened to Charlotte's request and suggested a decadent dessert.

After the band, a line of classic cars advanced from an expansive vacant lot.

Using Stressed and Unstressed Syllables: Long Vowels

1st syllable stressed

2nd syllable stressed

bracelet	achieve
explode	disease
icy	frozen
major	lazy
raccoon	pretend
reduce	recite

Bradley found it amusing to wear hideous, unsightly disguises and frighten people.

Mrs. David's class bided their time, waiting patiently for the distinguished athlete's visit.

Using Stressed and Unstressed Syllables: *R*-Controlled Vowels

1st syllable stressed

2nd syllable stressed

appear	alert
beware	article
dessert	compare
fearful	early
relearn	perfect
startle	sharpen

Mr. Becker's class was weary of rehearsing. Still, they were nervous about the performance.

Victoria's brother marred the walls with permanent marker. She was infuriated!

Prefixes

Introduction

Review prefixes. Then, write different prefixes on four sentence strips in large letters. Choose four students to hold each sentence strip across the front of the classroom. Write four roots in large letters on sentence strips that will create new words when combined with at least one of the chosen prefixes. Distribute them to seated students and ask them to line up behind the correct prefixes to make new words. Have the remaining students pronounce and define the new words.

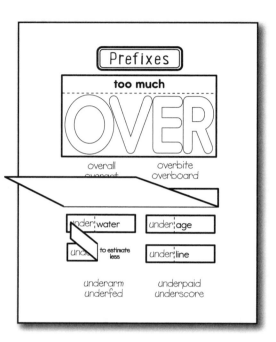

Creating the Notebook Page

Guide students through the following steps to complete the right-hand page in their notebooks.

1. Add a Table of Contents entry for the Prefixes pages.

2. Cut out the title and glue it to the top of the page.

3. Cut out the prefix flaps. Apply glue to the back of the top section of each flap and attach them to the page below the title. If desired, place each flap on its own page.

4. Cut out the word cards. Read the base word or root on each one. Then, write the prefix from one of the flaps on the left-hand side of the word card to create a new word. (Note: Some words can take multiple prefixes. Accept all correct words.) Apply glue to the back of the left section of the card and attach it under the correct prefix flap. Under each word flap, write the meaning of the new word.

5. Brainstorm more words that can be created with each prefix and write them on the page below the flaps. Or, use the page as a personal prefix dictionary and add related words to the page throughout the year as you come across them.

6. Use the blank template on page 51 to create pages for additional prefixes. Write a prefix on each large flap and write the meaning of the prefix on the top section of the flap. Write words that will make a complete word when used with the prefixes on the right sides of the word flaps.

Reflect on Learning

To complete the left-hand page, have students choose ten of the new words and use them to write a short story. Students should highlight the words with prefixes in their stories. Allow students to share their stories.

Prefixes

too much

OVER

below or less than

UNDER

line	due
achieve	age
estimate	water
look	night

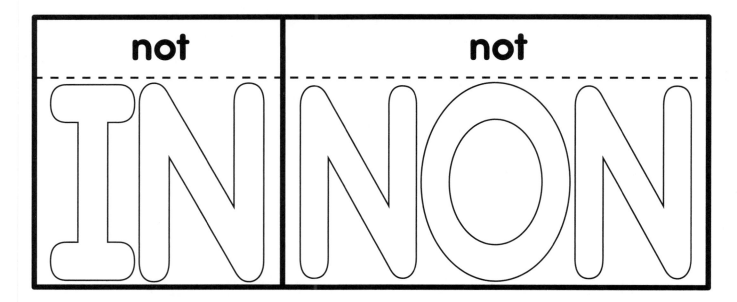

not **IN**   **not** **NON**

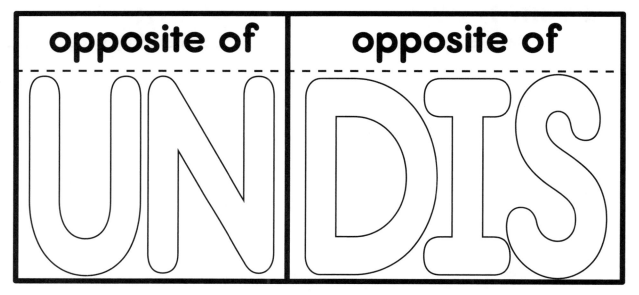

opposite of **UN**   **opposite of** **DIS**

	certain		sense
	active		loyal
	secure		agree
	usual		violent

again	before
RE	**PRE**

opposite; away	wrong
DE	**MIS**

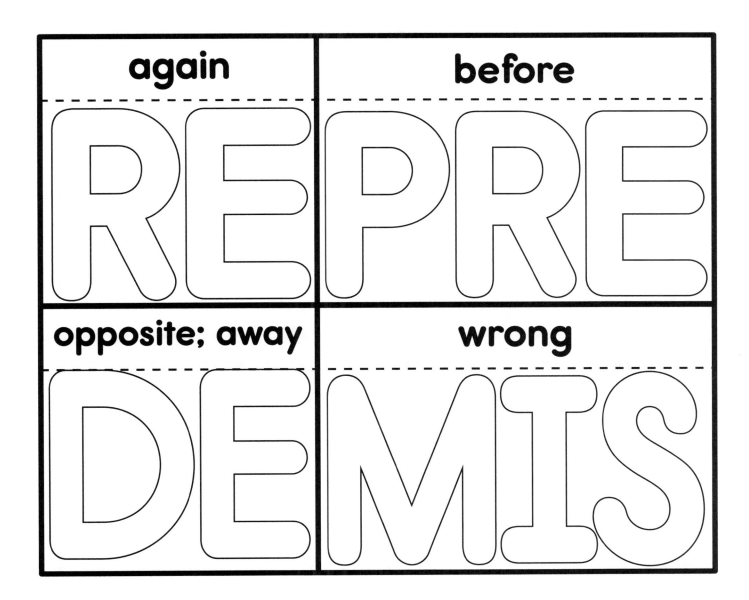

	frost		taken
	crease		vent
	connect		caution
	arrange		chief

one	three
UNI	TRI
two	four
BI	QUAD

son	cycle
focals	rant
que	ruple
cep	pod

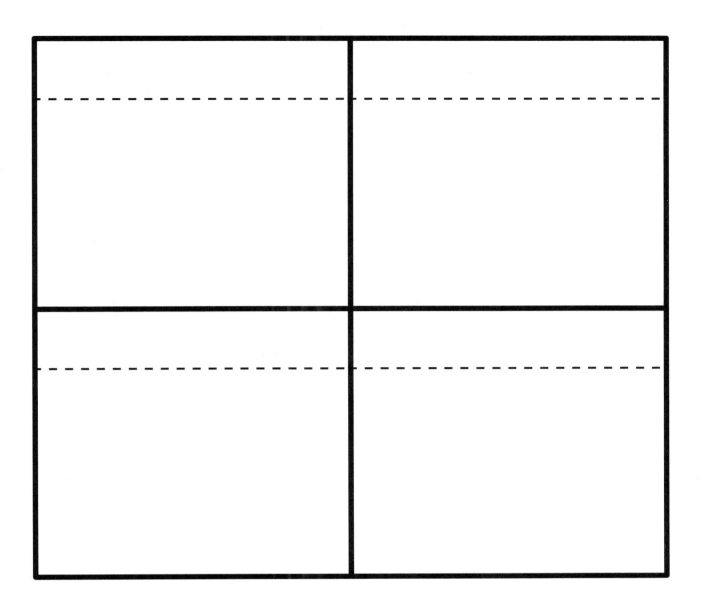

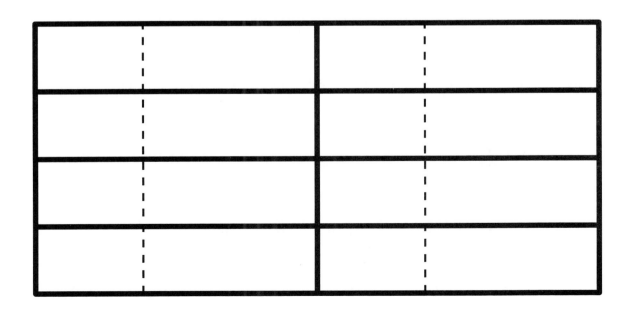

Suffixes

Introduction

Review suffixes. Have students find examples of words with suffixes in a book. Record the examples on the board, grouping them in lists by their suffixes. Discuss how the endings change on many of the roots or base words when a suffix is added to the word. Identify several examples from the lists on the board.

Creating the Notebook Page

Guide students through the following steps to complete the right-hand page in their notebooks.

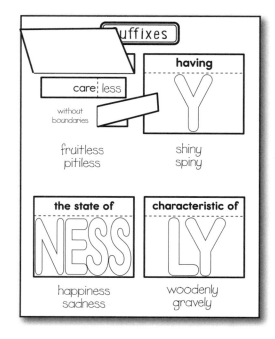

1. Add a Table of Contents entry for the Suffixes pages.

2. Cut out the title and glue it to the top of the page.

3. Cut out the suffix flaps. Apply glue to the back of the top section of each flap and attach them to the page below the title. If desired, place each flap on its own page.

4. Cut out the word cards. Read the base word or root on each one. Then, write the suffix from one of the flaps on the right-hand side of the word card to make a new word. (Note: Some words can take multiple suffixes. Accept all correct words.) Apply glue to the back of the right section of the card and attach it under the correct suffix flap. Under each word flap, write the meaning of the new word.

5. Brainstorm more words that can be created with each suffix and write them on the page below the flaps. Or, use the page as a personal suffix dictionary and add related words to the page throughout the year as you come across them.

6. Use the blank template on page 57 to create pages for additional suffixes. Write a suffix on each large flap and write the meaning of the suffix on the top section of the flap. Write words that will make a complete word when used with the suffixes on the left sides of the word flaps.

Reflect on Learning

To complete the left-hand page, distribute old magazines and newspapers to students and have them look for words with suffixes. Students should cut out the words and glue them to their page. Then, have students write the definitions of the words below each word.

Suffixes

having	the state of
Y	**NESS**
characteristic of	**without**
LY	**LESS**

mood		weak	
common		care	
firm		brave	
cream		bound	

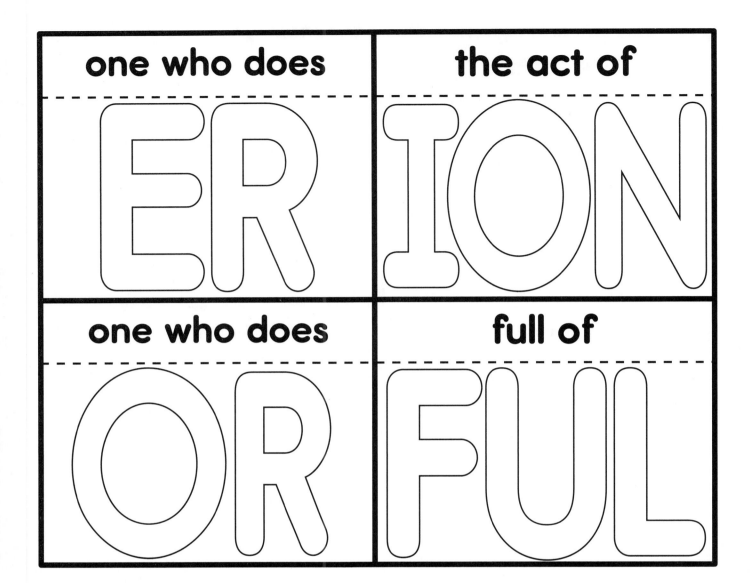

one who does	the act of
ER	**ION**
one who does	full of
OR	**FUL**

train	discuss
edit	elect
sail	respect
lead	flavor

can be done

ABLE

can be done

IBLE

act or state of

MENT

dispos

advertise

revers

commit

ed

destruct

amuse

break

aud

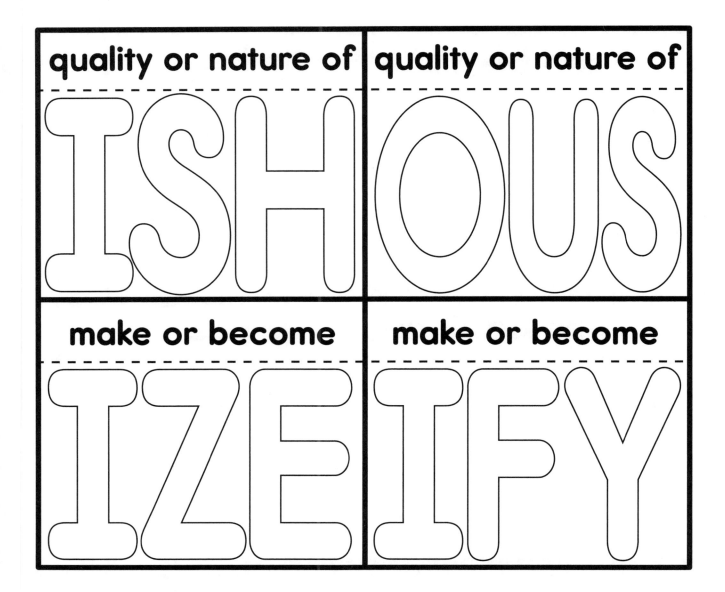

quality or nature of	quality or nature of
ISH	OUS

make or become	make or become
IZE	IFY

liqu	danger
child	visual
pur	fool
poison	alphabet

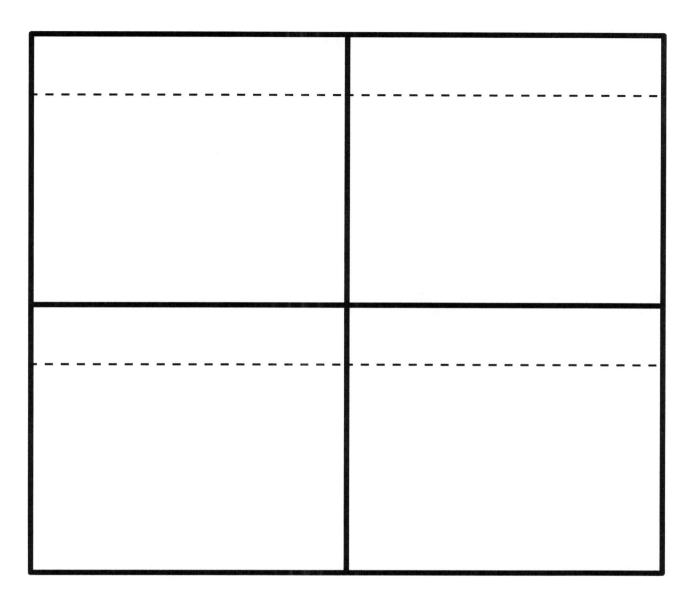

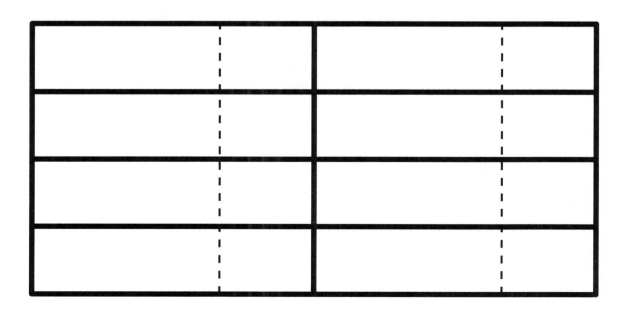

Suffixes **57**

Word Roots

Introduction

Write several words on the board that share the same root, such as *autofocus*, *autograph*, *automobile*, and *autobiography*. Have students point out what the words have in common. Then, have students share simple definitions for each word or look up the definitions in a dictionary. As a class, discuss how the definitions are similar. Finally, write a class definition for the root *auto* (self or same).

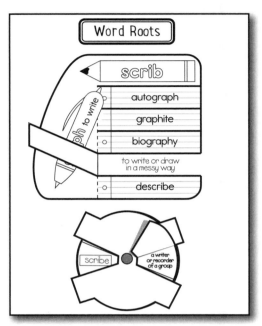

Creating the Notebook Page

Guide students through the following steps to complete the right-hand page in their notebooks.

1. Add a Table of Contents entry for the Word Roots pages.

2. Cut out the title and glue it to the top of the page.

3. Cut out the word root piece. Cut on the solid lines to create four or five flaps. Apply glue to the back of the root and definition section and attach it to the top of the page.

5. Discuss the meaning of the word root. Then, define each word under its flap.

6. Cut out the circles. On the circle with the tabs, cut on the solid lines to create a wedge-shaped flap. Push a brass paper fastener through the center dots of the circles to attach them so that the circle with the flap is on top. It may be helpful to create the hole in each piece separately first. Apply glue to the backs of the tabs on the top circle and attach it to the bottom of the page with the flap on the right side. Do not press the brass fastener through the page.

7. Spin the bottom circle so that the rectangles show in the left window. In each rectangle, write a word with that root. Lift the flap on the right window and write the definition of the word. Repeat with all four rectangles.

8. For practice, spin the bottom circle to show a word on the left side. Say the definition of the word. Lift the flap to see if you are correct.

9. Use the blank template on page 65 to create pages for additional word roots. Write the root and a short definition on the left section of the flap book. Write five words with that root on the flaps.

Reflect on Learning

To complete the left-hand page, have students use the word root(s) to create one or more new words. Students should define each new word and use it in a sentence.

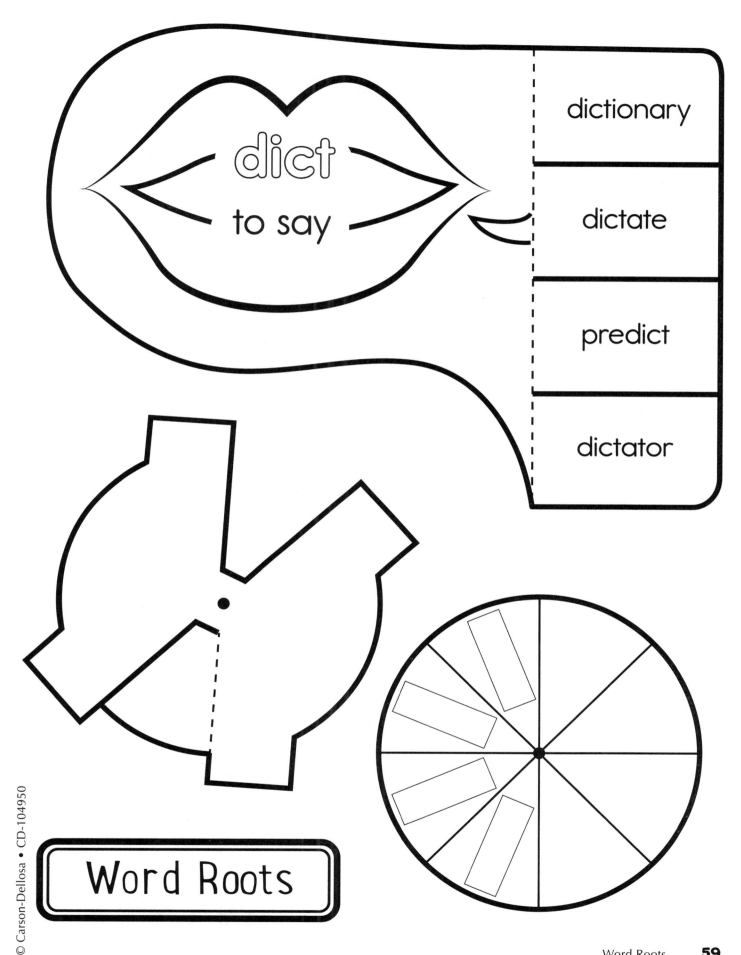

dict
to say

dictionary

dictate

predict

dictator

Word Roots

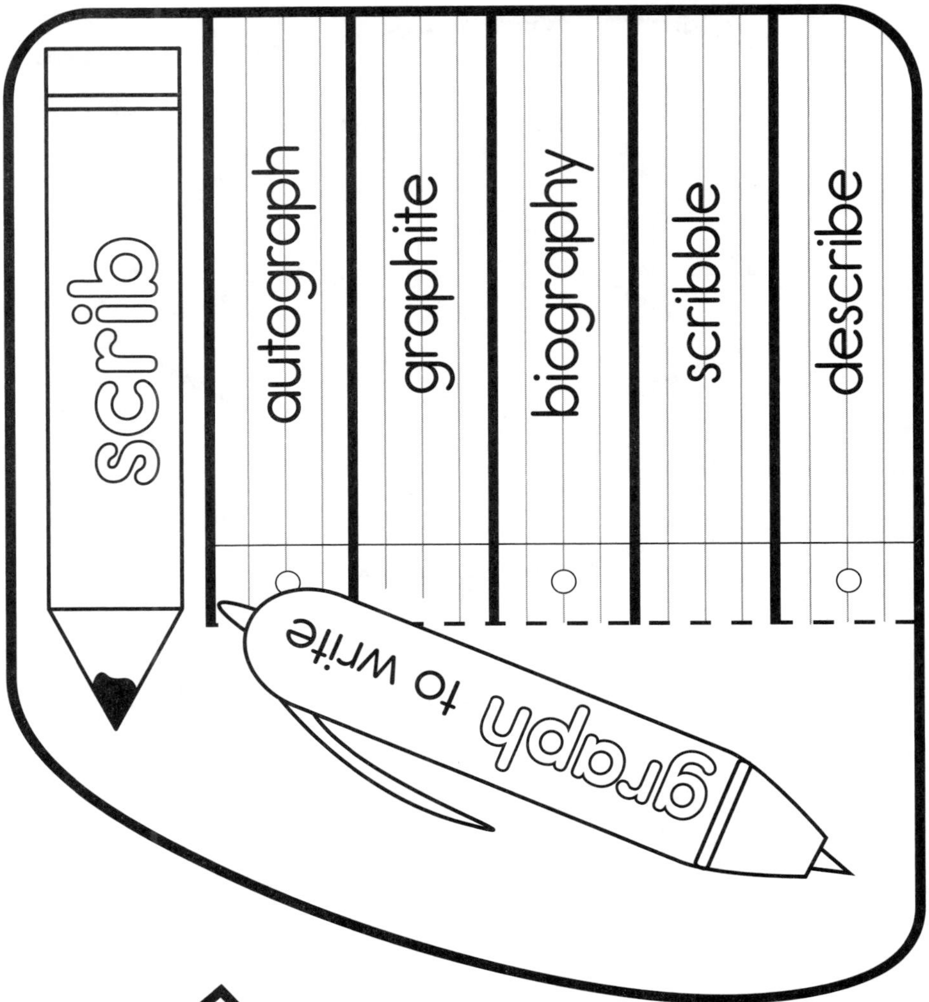

scrib

autograph

graphite

biography

scribble

describe

graph to write

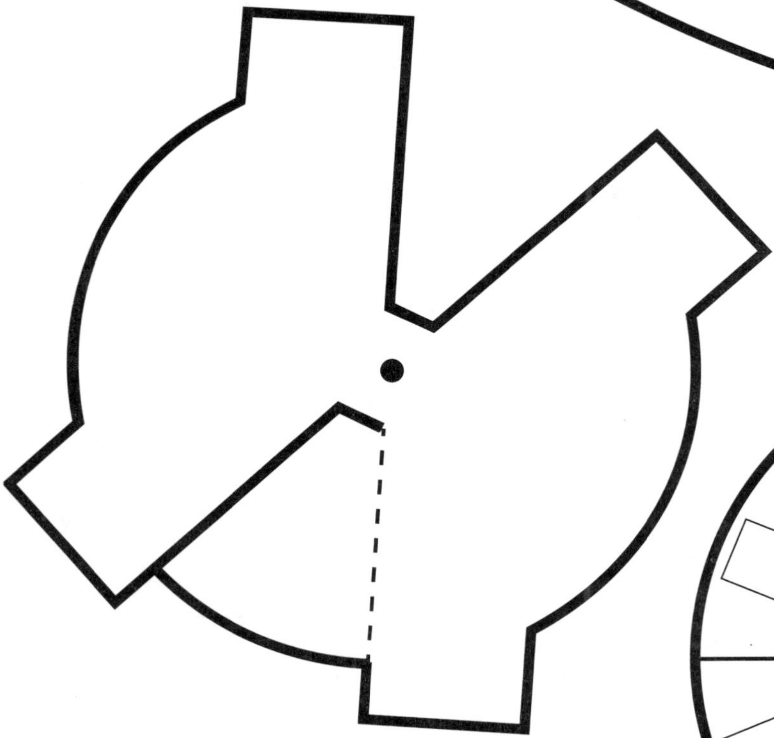

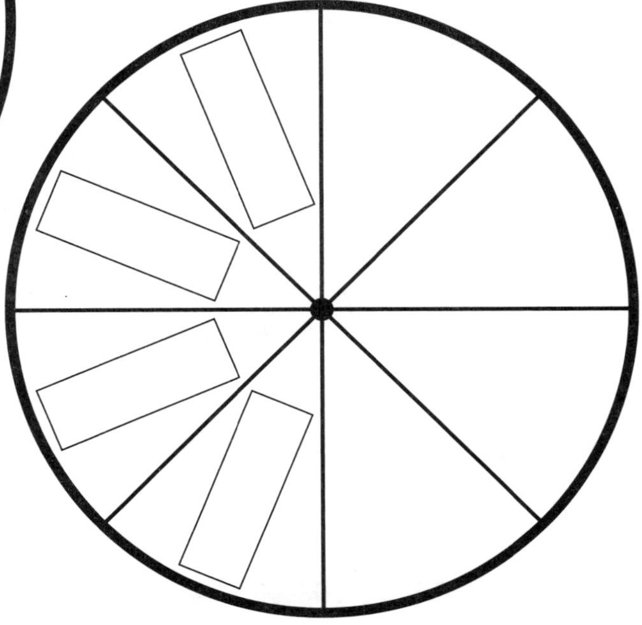

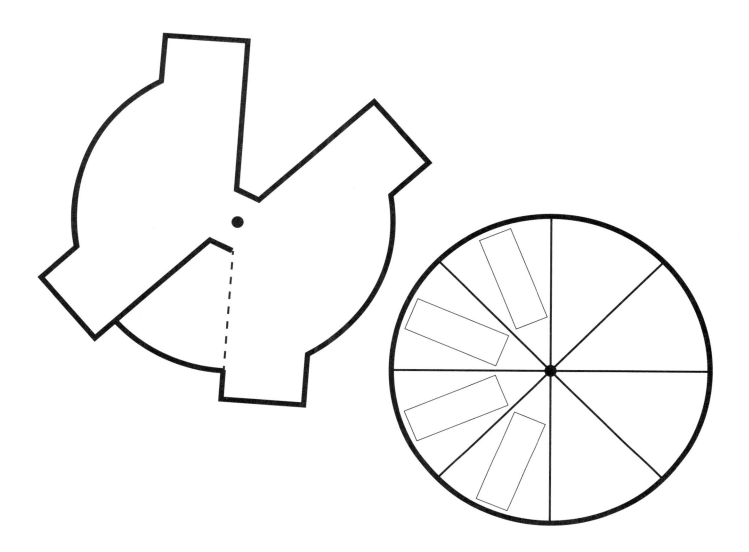

phon related to sound

microphone

phonetic

symphony

homophone

cacophony

Word Roots **61**

aquarium

aquatic

hydroelectric

hydrant

hydrate

related to water

hydra, aqua

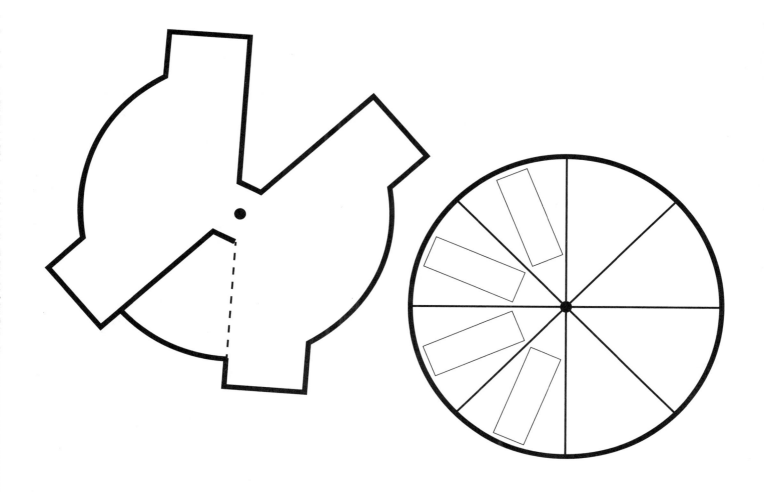

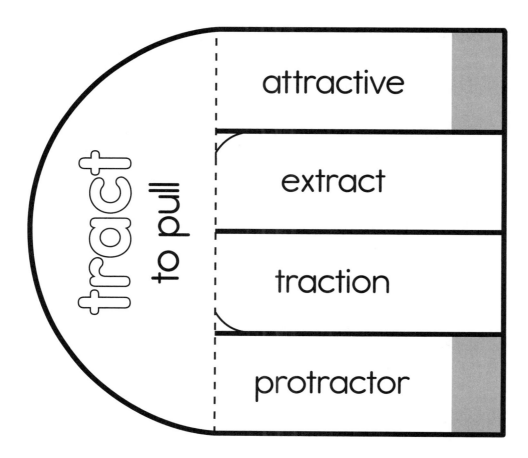

tract
to pull

attractive

extract

traction

protractor

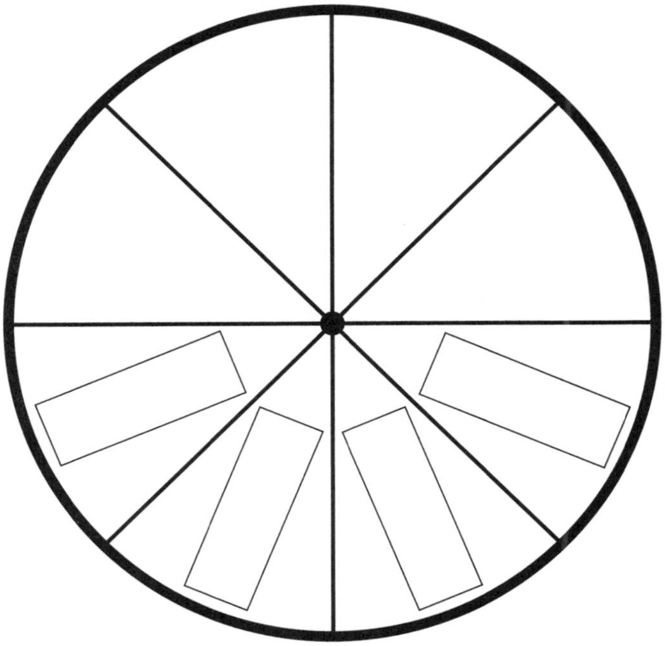

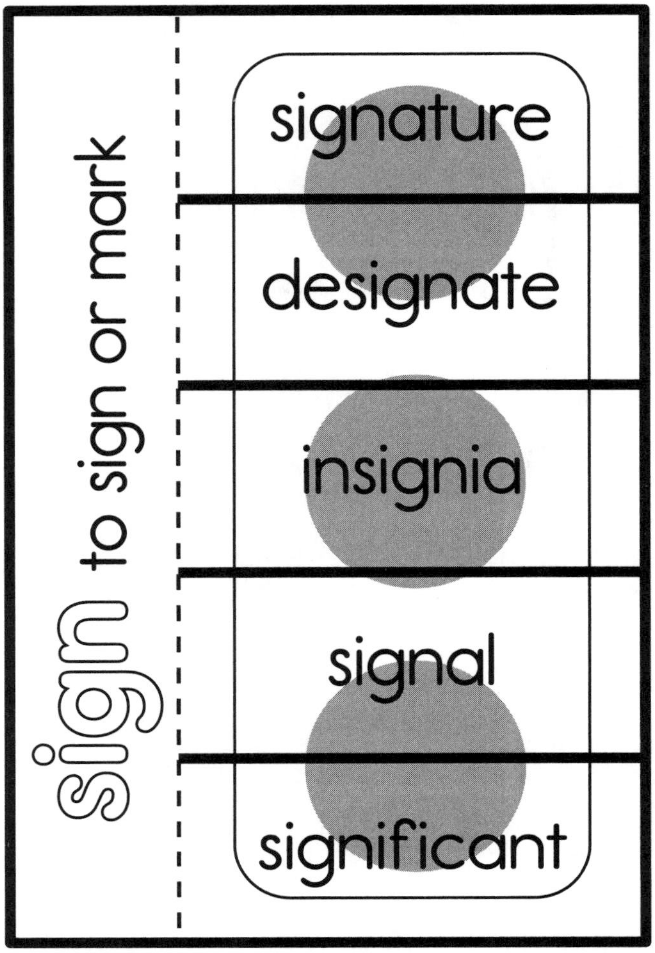

sign to sign or mark

signature

designate

insignia

signal

significant

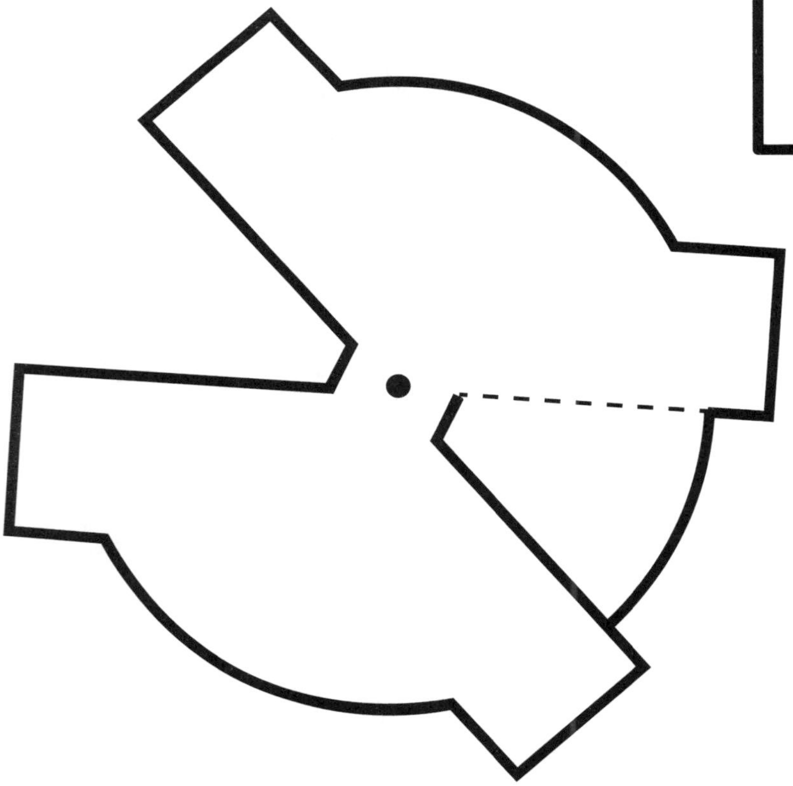

Using Affixes and Roots

Introduction

Review prefixes, roots, and suffixes using examples from science and social studies texts. Program several index cards with content-area vocabulary words that contain prefixes, roots, and suffixes such as *preamble*, *constitution*, and *amendment*. Distribute the cards and have students cut apart the index cards to separate each word part. On the backs of the cards, students should write the meaning of each word part. Have students exchange word parts to try to make other new words. Point out that once students are familiar with a root or affix, they can use that knowledge in multiple situations to expand their vocabulary.

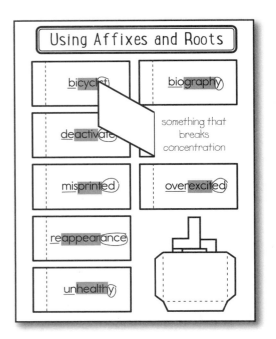

Creating the Notebook Page

Guide students through the following steps to complete the right-hand page in their notebooks.

1. Add a Table of Contents entry for the Using Affixes and Roots pages.

2. Cut out the title and glue it to the top of the page.

3. Cut out the "magnifying glass" piece. Cut on the solid lines to cut out the center rectangle. Apply glue to the front of the L-shaped flap and fold it over on the dashed line to seal the outer edge of the magnifying glass and create a handle.

4. Cut out the pocket. Apply glue to the backs of the three tabs and attach the pocket to the bottom-right side of the page. Store the magnifying glass in the pocket.

5. Cut out the flaps. Apply glue to the backs of the left sections and attach them to the page.

6. Read the word on each flap. Use the center of the magnifying glass to isolate parts of the word and find prefixes, roots, and suffixes. (Turn the magnifying glass horizontally or vertically to widen or reduce the visible area.) Divide the word into its word parts by circling and labeling them, or by using different colored highlighters.

7. Under the flap, write the definition of the word, using the affixes and roots as a clue to the meaning of the word.

Reflect on Learning

To complete the left-hand page, have students write a sentence using each of the words on the right-hand page. Students should highlight the word used in each sentence.

Using Affixes and Roots

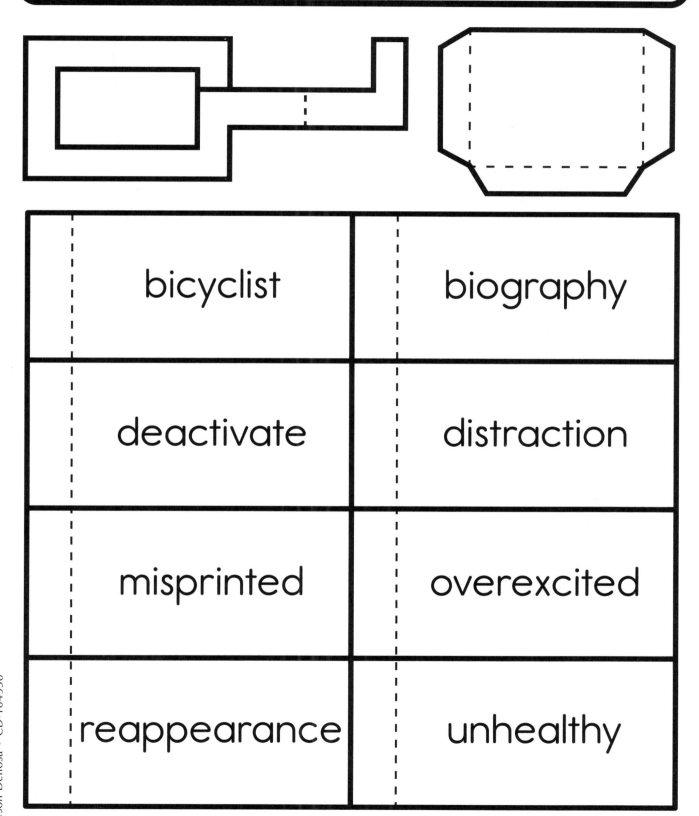

bicyclist	biography
deactivate	distraction
misprinted	overexcited
reappearance	unhealthy

Inflectional Endings

Introduction

Write a set of words on the board, such as *extends*, *extended*, and *extending*. Have students identify what is the same about each of them (the base word, *extend*). Explain that base words can take endings such as *-s, -es, -ed, -ing, -er,* and *-est* to change their meanings. Have students use the words in a sentence to show how the inflectional endings changed the meaning of the word *extend*.

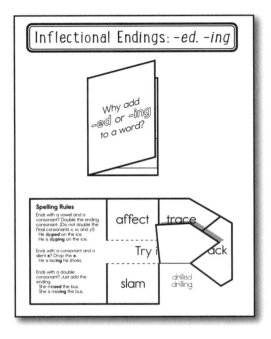

Creating the Notebook Page

Guide students through the following steps to complete the right-hand page in their notebooks.

1. Add a Table of Contents entry for the Inflectional Endings pages.

2. Cut out the title and glue it to the top of the page.

3. Cut out the *Why add . . .* piece and the arrow piece.

4. Complete the arrow(s). Complete the sentence(s) with the purpose of the inflectional ending, and then write an example word at the end of the arrow(s).

5. Fold the *Why add . . .* piece on the dashed line and then open it so that the blank side is faceup. Fold the sides on the arrow piece in on the dashed lines. Apply glue to the backs of the left and right sections. Place the arrow piece on top of the blank side of the *Why add* piece so that the left and right edges meet. Fold the piece closed like a book, pulling the center of the arrow piece out so it folds in half down the center to create a pop-up type book. Apply glue to the gray glue section on the back and attach it to the page below the title.

6. Cut out the *Spelling Rules* piece. Cut on the solid lines to create five flaps. Apply glue to the back of the left side and the narrow center section on the right and glue it to the bottom half of the page.

7. Read the spelling rules and examples. Read the word on each flap. Use the spelling rules to change the ending for each word. Write the new words under the flaps.

Reflect on Learning

To complete the left-hand page, have students prove each spelling rule by finding and recording more examples. It may be helpful to encourage students look through a dictionary or a book to find examples.

Inflectional Endings: -s, -es

Why add -s or -es to a word?

glue

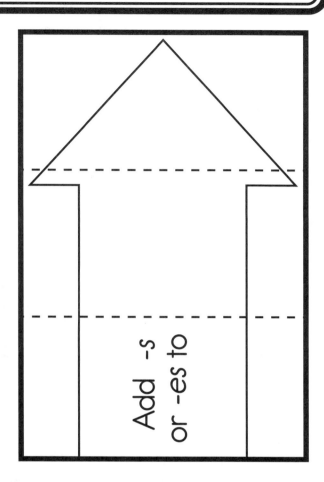

Add -s or -es to

Spelling Rules

For most third-person singular (he, she, it) verbs, add -**s**.
  She jump**s** on the bed.

Does it end with the letters **s**, **z**, **sh**, **ch**, or **x**? Add -**es**.
  He fix**es** his lunch every day.

Ends with a consonant + **y**?
Change **y** to **i** and add -**es**.
  He always tri**es** to do his best.

study

polish

Try it!

lunge

create

carry

Inflectional Endings: -ed, -ing

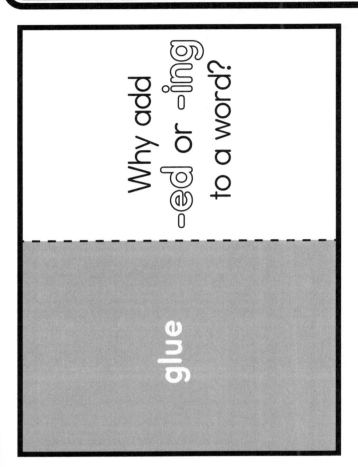

Why add
-ed or -ing
to a word?

glue

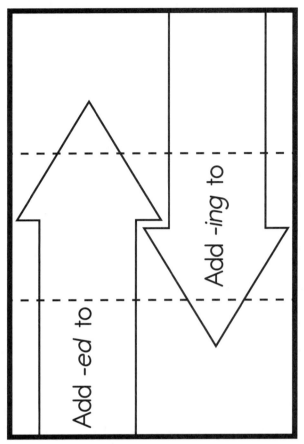

Add -ed to

Add -ing to

Spelling Rules

Ends with a vowel and a consonant? Double the ending consonant. (Do not double the final consonants *x*, *w*, and *y*!)
He slip**ped** on the ice.
He is slip**ping** on the ice.

Ends with a consonant and a silent **e**? Drop the **e**.
He is lac**ing** his shoes.

Ends with a double consonant? Just add the ending.
She mis**sed** the bus.
She is mis**sing** the bus.

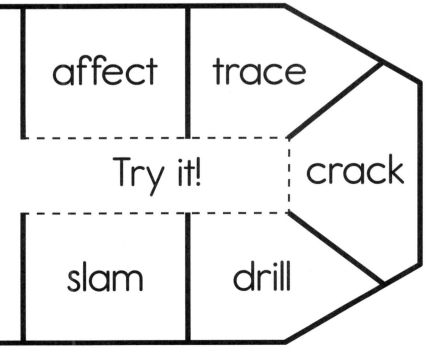

affect

trace

Try it!

crack

slam

drill

Inflectional Endings: -er, -est

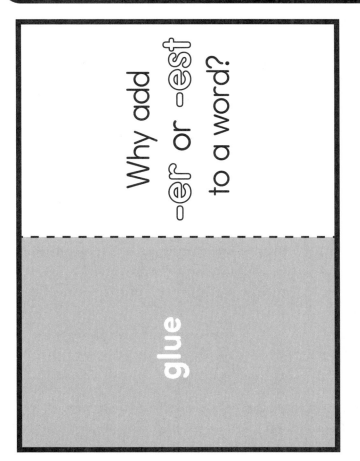

Why add -er or -est to a word?

glue

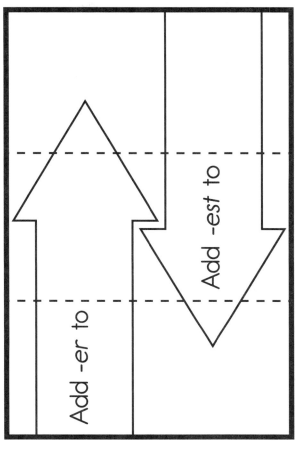

Add -er to

Add -est to

Spelling Rules

Ends with a silent **e**? Drop the **e**.
My cat is cut**er** than her turtle.
My puppy is the cut**est** pet.

Ends with a **y**? Change the **y** to **i**.
The flowers are prett**ier** in the spring.
The flowers are prett**iest** in the morning.

Ends with a vowel and a consonant? Double the ending consonant. (Do not double the final consonants x, w, or y!)
Her pencil is thin**ner** than mine.
You have the thin**nest** pencil.

dirty

noisy

Try it!

hot

safe

wise

Plural Nouns

Introduction

Review a noun as a word that names a person, place, thing, or idea. Explain that nouns can be singular and name one thing, or they can be plural and name more than one thing. Review how most nouns can be made plural by adding -s to the end of the word as in *grades*, *skateboards*, and *snacks*. Explain how some words are a little trickier. Review the plural noun rules for this lesson. Brainstorm other words that follow each rule and list them on the board.

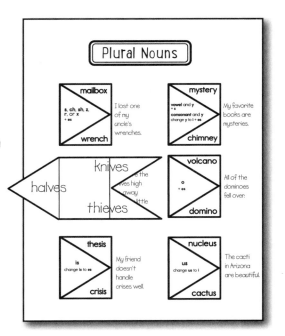

Creating the Notebook Page

Guide students through the following steps to complete the right-hand page in their notebooks.

1. Add a Table of Contents entry for the Plural Nouns pages.

2. Cut out the title and glue it to the top of the page.

3. Cut out the flap books.

4. With each piece blank side up, fold the flaps toward the center on the dashed lines. Apply glue to the gray glue sections on the back and attach them to the page, leaving enough room to write a sentence on the page below or beside each flap.

5. Read each spelling rule. Then, write the correct plural ending for each word under the flap. Under the center flap, write a new plural noun using the corresponding spelling rule.

6. Below or beside each piece, write a sentence using one of the plural nouns listed on the flaps.

Reflect on Learning

To complete the left-hand page, write several more nouns on the board. Have students copy each noun, draw an arrow, and then write the correct plural form of the word.

Plural Nouns

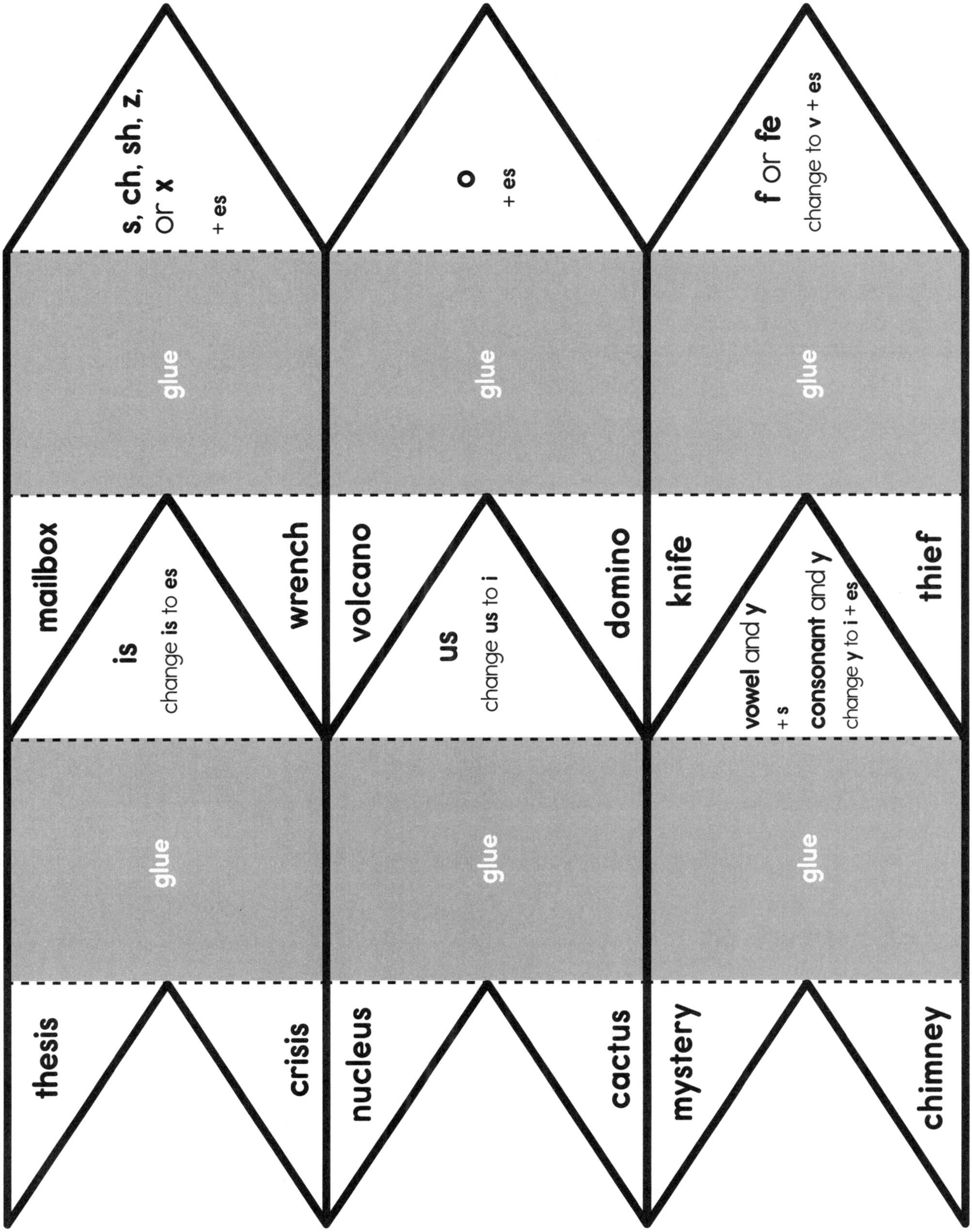

s, ch, sh, z,
or **x**
+ **es**

o
+ **es**

f or **fe**
change to **v** + **es**

glue

glue

glue

mailbox

wrench

is
change **is** to **es**

volcano

domino

us
change **us** to **i**

knife

thief

vowel and y
+ **s**

consonant and y
change y to i + **es**

glue

glue

glue

thesis

crisis

nucleus

cactus

mystery

chimney

Homographs

Introduction

Write a homograph on the board, such as *wave*. Ask a volunteer to define the word *wave* and use it in a sentence. Then, have another volunteer give another definition of *wave* and use it in a sentence. Explain that homographs are words that are spelled the same but may have different meanings and may or may not sound the same. Write other homographs on the board, such as *tear* and *scale,* and have students use them in sentences to demonstrate that they understand the different meanings of the words.

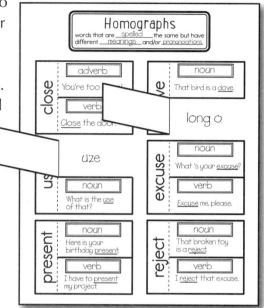

Creating the Notebook Page

Guide students through the following steps to complete the right-hand page in their notebooks.

1. Add a Table of Contents entry for the Homographs pages.

2. Cut out the title and glue it to the top of the page.

3. Complete the definition (words that are **spelled** the same but have different **meanings** and/or **pronunciations**).

4. Cut out the flap books. Cut on the solid line to create two flaps on each one. Apply glue to the backs of the left sections and attach them to the page.

5. In the two blank boxes, write the two parts of speech for the word on the flap. For example, *close* is an adverb and a verb. Then, write a short example sentence for each part of speech such as, *You're too close!* (adverb) or *Close the door.* (verb).

6. Under each flap, write a clue for the pronunciation of the word (for example, "cloh-s" and "cloze" or "REject" and "reJECT").

Reflect on Learning

To complete the left-hand page, brainstorm more homographs with students and list them on the board. Then, have each student choose four homographs. For each homograph, students should draw a picture to illustrate the word's meaning and write a sentence with the word. Finally, students should give the part of speech for the word.

Homographs

words that are _____ the same but have different _____ and/or _____

close		dove	
	☐		☐
	☐		☐

use		excuse	
	☐		☐
	☐		☐

present		reject	
	☐		☐
	☐		☐

Homophones

Introduction

Say the following silly sentence aloud: *Peter ate eight pairs of pears as he set sail on the boat he bought on sale.* Discuss which words sound the same and how students understood the meaning anyway. Record the word pairs on the board. Have students volunteer more homophone pairs. Point out the different spellings and meanings in each pair. Explain that words that sound the same but are spelled differently and have different meanings are called homophones, and they can be tricky to spell correctly.

Creating the Notebook Page

Guide students through the following steps to complete the right-hand page in their notebooks.

1. Add a Table of Contents entry for the Homophones pages.

2. Cut out the title and glue it to the top of the page.

3. Complete the definition (words that **sound** the same but have different **spellings** and **meanings**).

4. Cut out the flap books. Cut on the solid lines to create five flaps on each one. Apply glue to the back of the left and right sections and attach them side-by-side on the page so that the edges of the flaps meet in the center.

5. On each flap, write or draw a clue below the word to help you remember the meaning.

6. Under each pair of flaps, write a sentence using both of the homophones. If desired, shade each homophone pair a different color to clearly define the pairs.

Reflect on Learning

To complete the left-hand page, brainstorm more homophone pairs on the board with the class. Have students write a silly story using as many homophones as possible, taking care to use and spell each one correctly.

Homophones

words that _____ the same but have different _____ and _____

allowed	aloud
passed	past
threw	through
weather	whether
who's	whose

Tabs

Cut out each tab and label it. Apply glue to the back of each tab and align it on the outside edge of the page with only the label section showing beyond the edge. Then, fold each tab to seal the page inside.

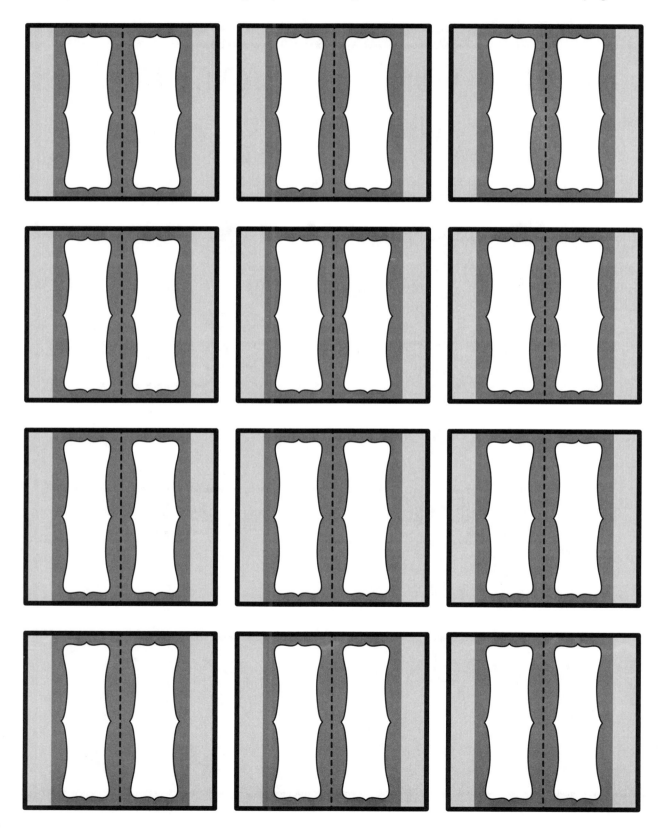

Cut out the KWL chart and cut on the solid lines to create three separate flaps. Apply glue to the back of the Topic section to attach the chart to a notebook page.

Topic:

What I

Know

What I

Wonder

What I

Learned

Library Pocket

Cut out the library pocket on the solid lines. Fold in the side tabs and apply glue to them before folding up the front of the pocket. Apply glue to the back of the pocket to attach it to a notebook page.

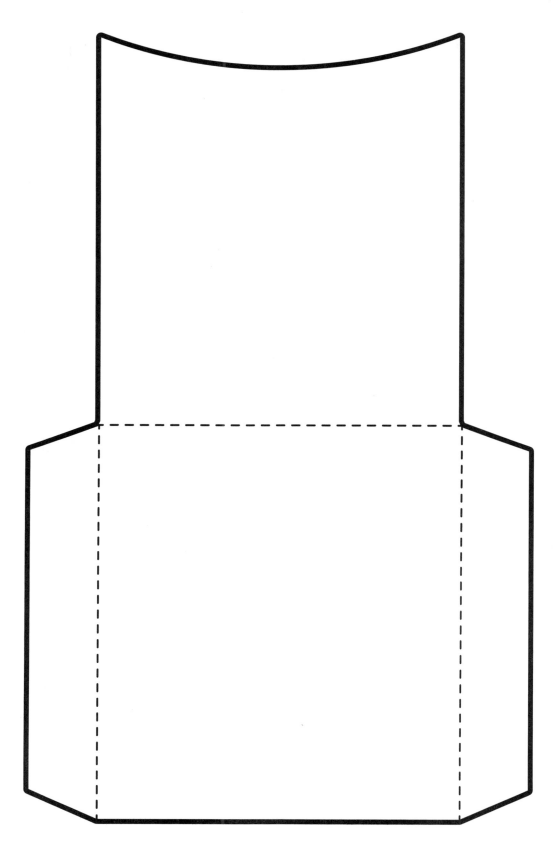

Envelope

Cut out the envelope on the solid lines. Fold in the side tabs and apply glue to them before folding up the rectangular front of the envelope. Fold down the triangular flap to close the envelope. Apply glue to the back of the envelope to attach it to a notebook page.

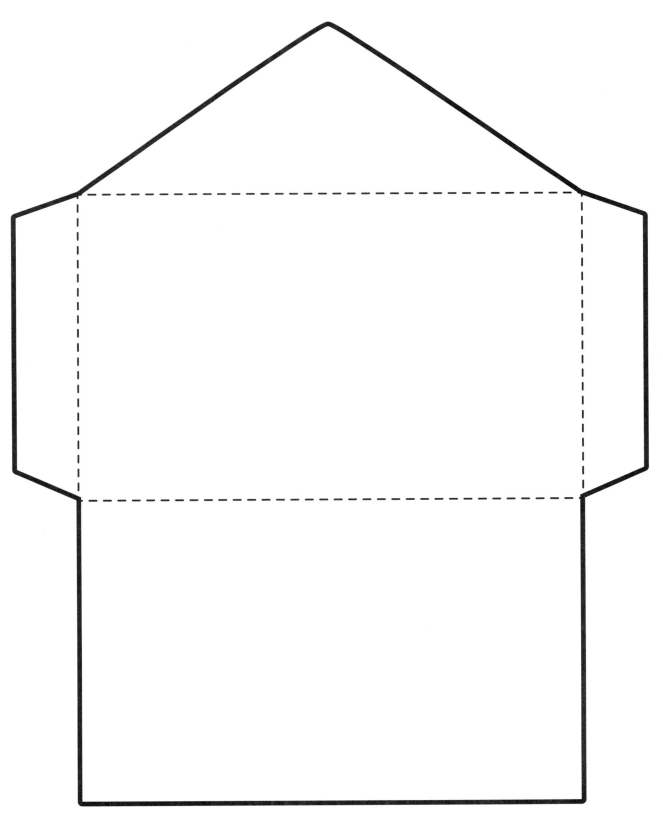

Pocket and Cards

Cut out the pocket on the solid lines. Fold over the front of the pocket. Then, apply glue to the tabs and fold them around the back of the pocket. Apply glue to the back of the pocket to attach it to a notebook page. Cut out the cards and store them in the envelope.

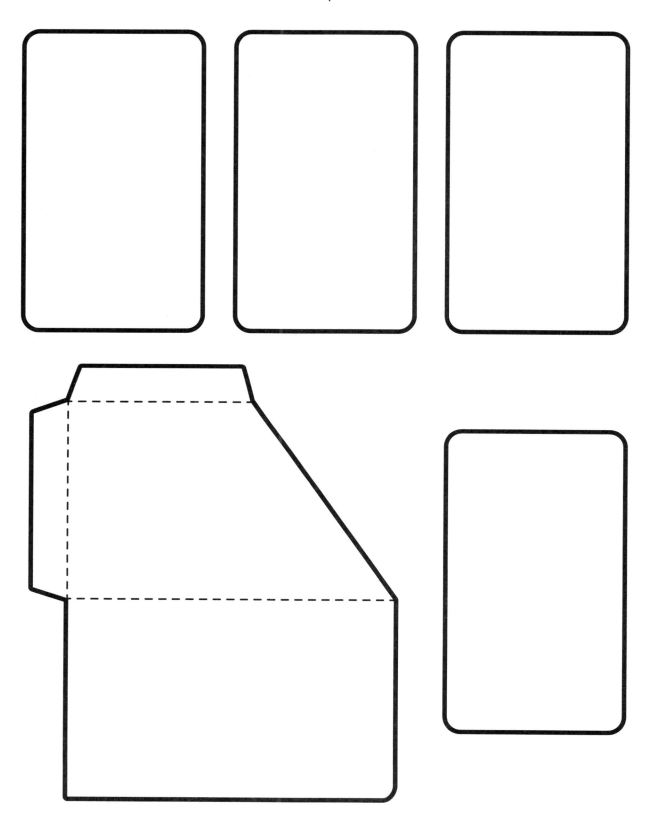

Six-Flap Shutter Fold

Cut out the shutter fold around the outside border. Then, cut on the solid lines to create six flaps. Fold the flaps toward the center. Apply glue to the back of the shutter fold to attach it to a notebook page.

If desired, this template can be modified to create a four-flap shutter fold by cutting off the bottom row. You can also create two three-flap books by cutting it in half down the center line.

Eight-Flap Shutter Fold

Cut out the shutter fold around the outside border. Then, cut on the solid lines to create eight flaps. Fold the flaps toward the center. Apply glue to the back of the shutter fold to attach it to a notebook page.

If desired, this template can be modified to create two four-flap shutter folds by cutting off the bottom two rows. You can also create two four-flap books by cutting it in half down the center line.

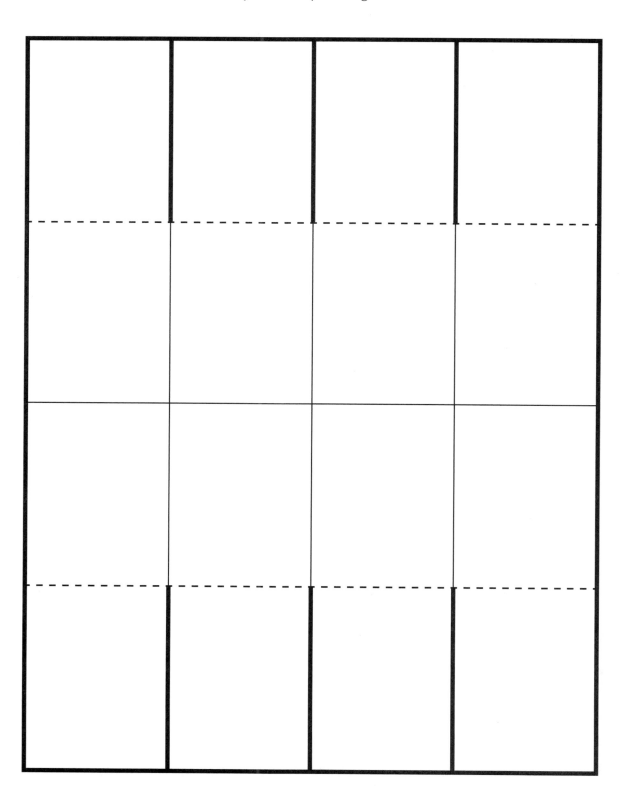

Flap Book—Eight Flaps

Cut out the flap book around the outside border. Then, cut on the solid lines to create eight flaps. Apply glue to the back of the center section to attach it to a notebook page.

If desired, this template can be modified to create a six-flap or two four-flap books by cutting off the bottom row or two. You can also create a tall four-flap book by cutting off the flaps on the left side.

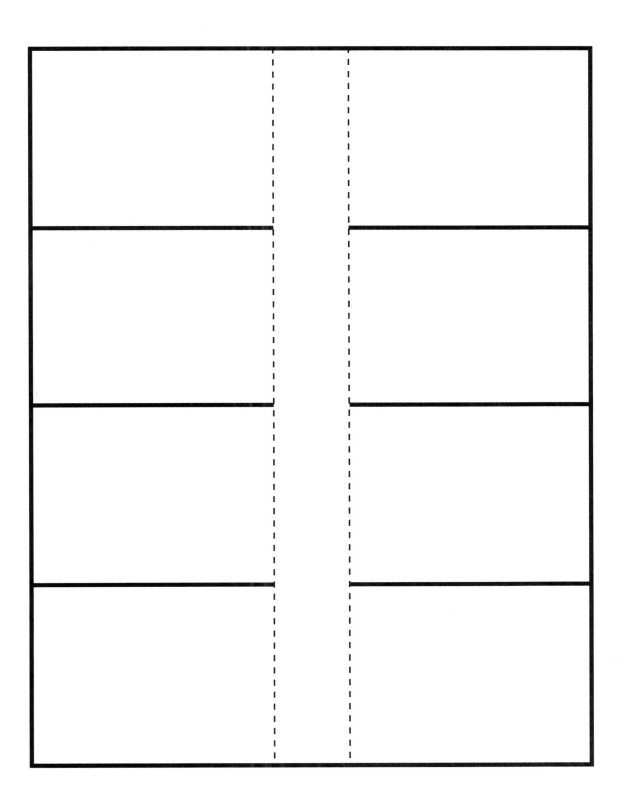

Flap Book—Twelve Flaps

Cut out the flap book around the outside border. Then, cut on the solid lines to create 12 flaps. Apply glue to the back of the center section to attach it to a notebook page.

If desired, this template can be modified to create smaller flap books by cutting off any number of rows from the bottom. You can also create a tall flap book by cutting off the flaps on the left side.

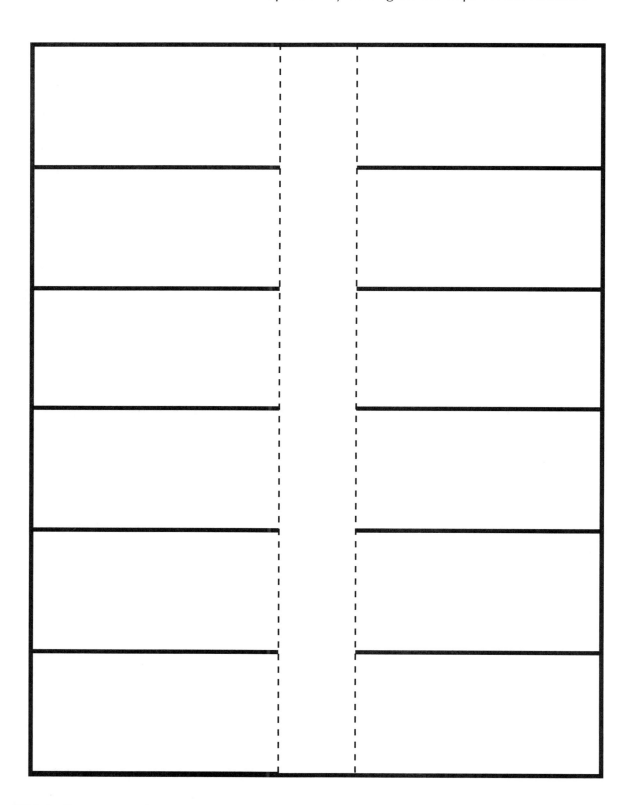

Interlocking Booklet

Cut out the booklet on the solid lines, including the short vertical lines on the top and bottom flaps. Then, fold the top and bottom flaps toward the center, interlocking them using the small vertical cuts. Apply glue to the back of the center panel to attach it to a notebook page.

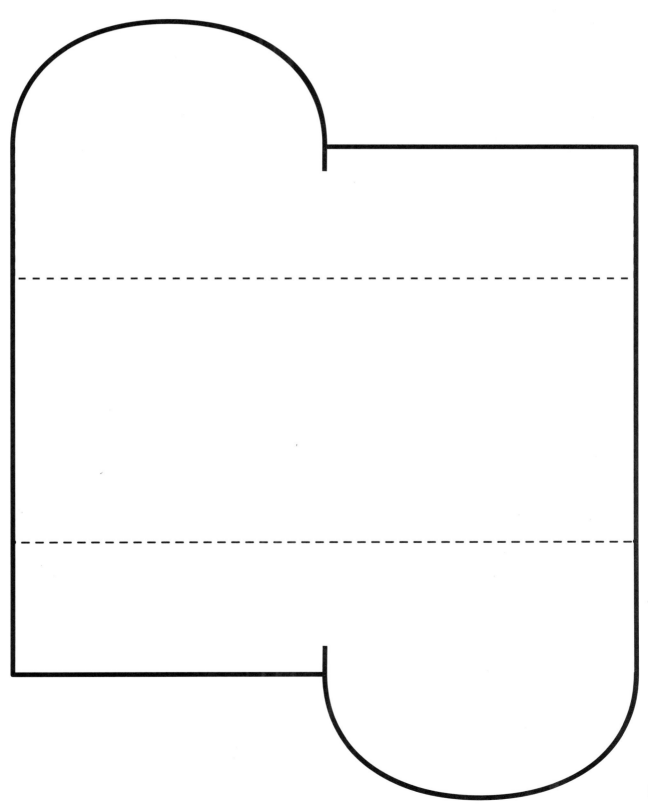

Four-Flap Petal Fold

Cut out the shape on the solid lines. Then, fold the flaps toward the center. Apply glue to the back of the center panel to attach it to a notebook page.

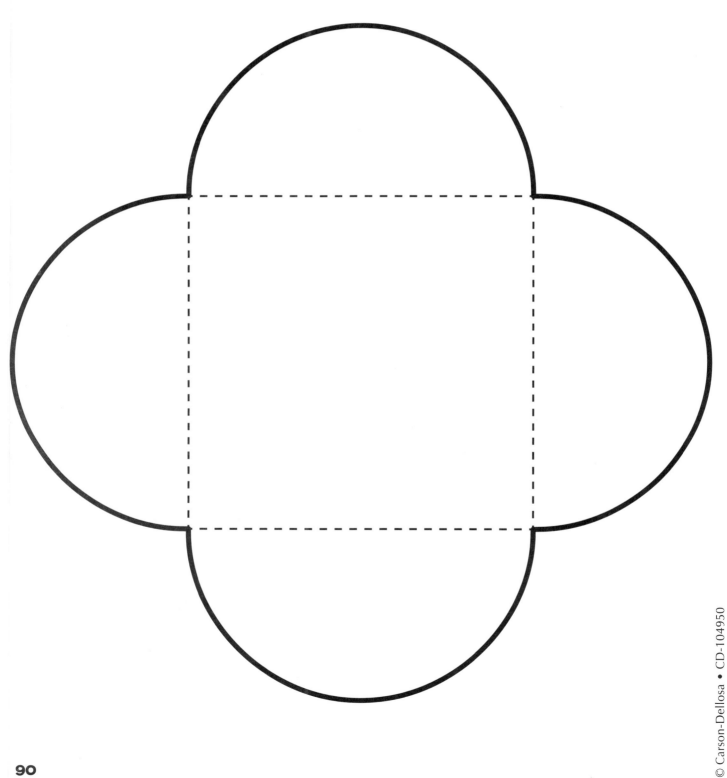

Six-Flap Petal Fold

Cut out the shape on the solid lines. Then, fold the flaps toward the center and back out. Apply glue to the back of the center panel to attach it to a notebook page.

Accordion Folds

Cut out the accordion pieces on the solid lines. Fold on the dashed lines, alternating the fold direction. Apply glue to the back of the last section to attach it to a notebook page.

You may modify the accordion books to have more or fewer pages by cutting off extra pages or by having students glue the first and last panels of two accordion books together.

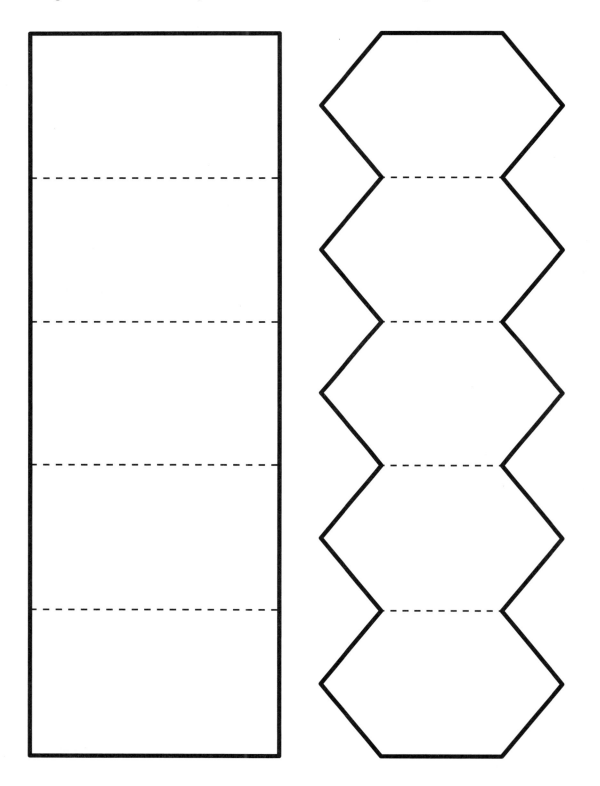

Accordion Folds

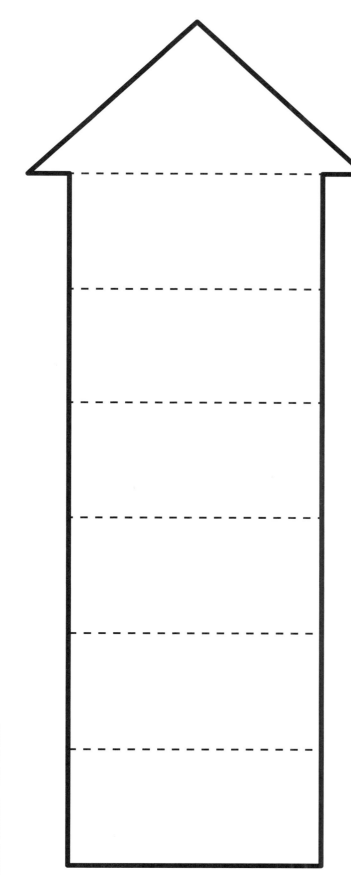

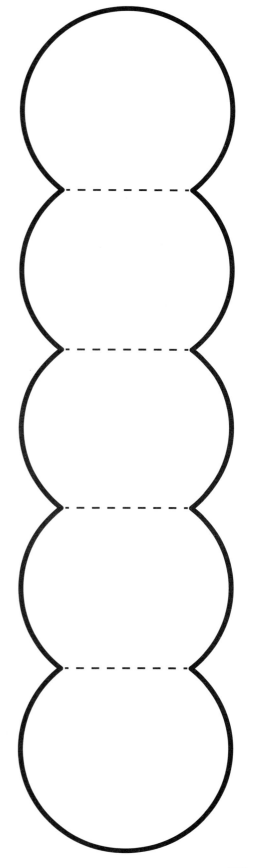

Clamshell Fold

Cut out the clamshell fold on the solid lines. Fold and unfold the piece on the three dashed lines. With the piece oriented so that the folds form an X with a horizontal line through it, pull the left and right sides together at the fold line. Then, keeping the sides touching, bring the top edge down to meet the bottom edge. You should be left with a triangular shape that unfolds into a square. Apply glue to the back of the triangle to attach the clamshell to a notebook page.

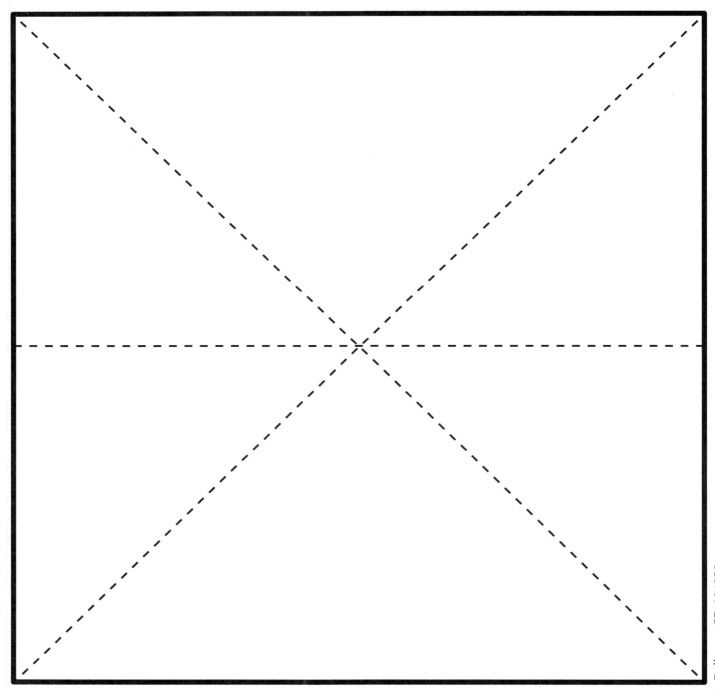

Cut out each puzzle along the solid lines to create a three- or four-piece puzzle. Apply glue to the back of each puzzle piece to attach it to a notebook page. Alternatively, apply glue only to one edge of each piece to create flaps.

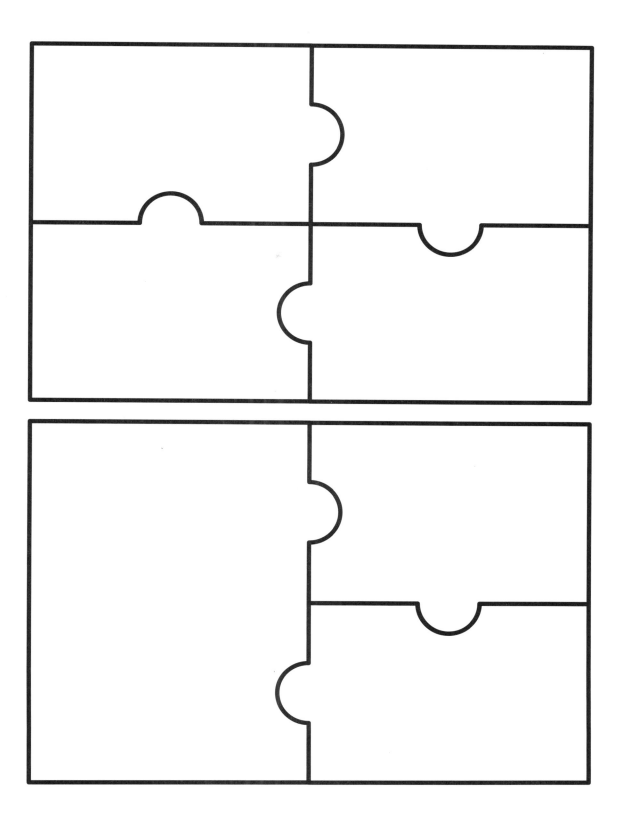

Flip Book

Cut out the two rectangular pieces on the solid lines. Fold each rectangle on the dashed lines. Fold the piece with the gray glue section so that it is inside the fold. Apply glue to the gray glue section and place the other folded rectangle on top so that the folds are nested and create a book with four cascading flaps. Make sure that the inside pages are facing up so that the edges of both pages are visible. Apply glue to the back of the book to attach it to a notebook page.

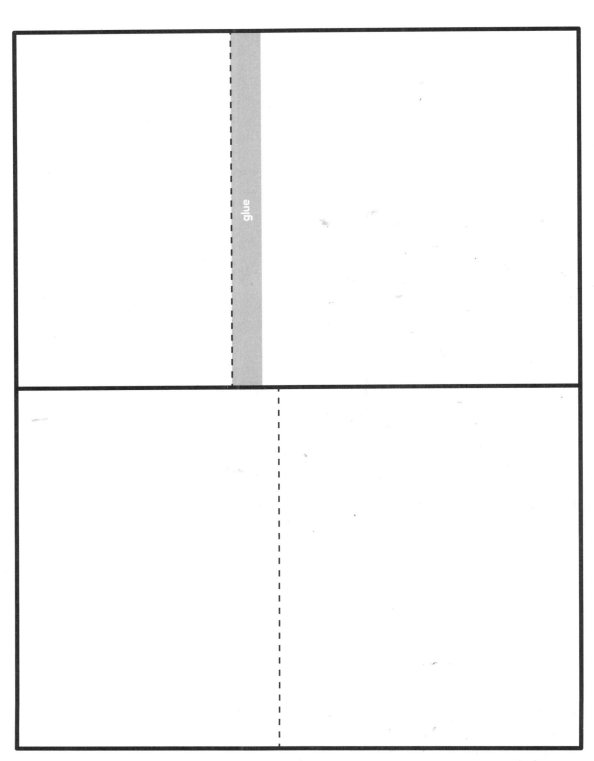